M000304382

EXPERIENCING MOUNT VERNON

Experiencing
MOUNT VERNON

EYEWITNESS ACCOUNTS, 1784–1865

Edited by Jean B. Lee

UNIVERSITY OF VIRGINIA PRESS

Charlottesville and London

University of Virginia Press
© 2006 by the Rector and Visitors of the University of Virginia
All rights reserved
Printed in the United States of America on acid-free paper
FIRST PUBLISHED 2006

9 8 7 6 5 4 3 2 1

Library of Congress Cataloging-in-Publication Data
Experiencing Mount Vernon : eyewitness accounts, 1784–1865 / edited by Jean B. Lee
p.   cm.
Includes bibliographical references and index.
ISBN 0-8139-2514-2 (cloth : alk. paper) — ISBN 0-8139-2515-0 (pbk. : alk. paper)
1. Mount Vernon (Va. : Estate) 2. Washington, George, 1732–1799—Homes and haunts—
Virginia—Mount Vernon (Estate)   I. Lee, Jean Butenhoff.
E312.5.E97 2006
975.5'291—dc22

2005030652

TITLE PAGE IMAGE: A bird's-eye view of Mount Vernon.
Lithograph produced by H. Whately and T. Sinclair, 1859.
(Courtesy of the Mount Vernon Ladies' Association)

For Merrill D. Peterson

Go to Mount Vernon, every one who can. It will reward you well.

—ANONYMOUS, 1865

I felt grateful for the privilege of visiting this consecrated spot,
and thought I could not fully enjoy the present, but what a glorious
reminiscence it would be when at home, when the excitement had
passed and left the deep, calm impression upon my memory.

—CAROLINE MOORE, 1833

CONTENTS

CONTENTS

If one stands in front of the mansion at Mount Vernon and casts an eye across the broad Potomac, on the distant southeastern horizon is a jut of land, part of Charles County, Maryland. My own journey to Mount Vernon began there, during research for my first book. In the 1770s George Washington, through a court case involving a debt, came into possession of a plantation and a slave in the county, and he ordered that the slave be removed to his estate. In the course of finding out what happened to that man, I discovered the stunning richness of the documentary and material evidence for eighteenth-century Mount Vernon, which became my next major research project. Such endeavors have a way of taking on a life of their own, of leading the researcher in unanticipated directions, and after a few years of work I expanded the investigation into the nineteenth century, as far as the end of the Civil War.

Several interpretive essays are now in print, and more publications will follow, including a book on the problems of slavery at Mount Vernon during the lifetimes of George and Martha Washington.[1] The current volume gathers together the best, most informative and evocative, of over one hundred accounts written by people who visited the estate between 1785 and 1865. Complementing these accounts are a few documents written by those who owned the property between the Revolution and the Civil War. In addition, visual images, many dating from the years 1783 to 1865, contain important information about what people experienced at the site.

In preparing this volume for publication, I have provided an explanatory headnote for each document, as well as brief annotations that identify references in the text. The latter have been kept to a minimum in order not to intrude unnecessarily on the contemporary voices. So too for editorial emendations of the texts, which are employed only where required to clarify meaning and are indicated with square brackets. Some items of interest to visitors (for example, the key to the Bastille, which Lafayette sent to Washington as a token of the early French Revolution) generated numerous and redundant descriptions; in such cases some repetitious passages have been omitted and so indicated with ellipses.

The following abbreviations have been employed in the notes:

BW   Bushrod Washington
GW   George Washington
MVLA   Mount Vernon Ladies' Association of the Union

Note

1. Jean B. Lee, "Mount Vernon Plantation: A Model for the Republic," in *Slavery at the Home of George Washington,* ed. Philip J. Schwarz (Mount Vernon, Va.: Mount Vernon Ladies' Association, 2001), 12–45; Lee, "Historical Memory, Sectional Strife, and the American Mecca: Mount Vernon, 1783–1853," *Virginia Magazine of History and Biography* 109 (2001): 255–300; Lee, "Jane C. Washington, Family, and Nation at Mount Vernon, 1830–55," in *Women Shaping the South: Creating and Confronting Change,* ed. Angela Boswell and Judith McArthur (Columbia: University of Missouri Press, 2005); Lee, *The Problems of Slavery at Mount Vernon, 1783–1802* (forthcoming).

ACKNOWLEDGMENTS

Like eighteenth- and nineteenth-century visitors to Mount Vernon, I have vivid memories of my time there. Foremost among them are many days spent in the library, where my intense focus on source materials occasionally was interrupted by the sounds of guinea hens just outside or, in the distance, the sight of mules grazing in a field. Equally vivid are memories of strolling the grounds, whether on one of those glorious April days in Virginia when the dogwoods, azaleas, and redbuds are all in bloom, or on a windy January day crowned by a somber sky, a time when it is not difficult to imagine people huddled near fireplaces during winters long past. Experiencing Mount Vernon has been essential to my understanding of this unique place.

Beside memories of place are those of people associated with it; they have encouraged my research in countless ways. I thought I was working on the eighteenth-century estate until Barbara A. McMillan suggested that I have a look at the nineteenth-century documents. That led to several additional years of research, which revealed the immense symbolic value that Americans imparted to Mount Vernon between 1800 and the Civil War, and to some of the most exciting research discoveries during my career as a historian. For this expanded focus, and for the many ways in which she accommodated my research needs, I owe Dr. McMillan a special measure of gratitude. So too with Mary V. Thompson, who generously shared her unmatched knowledge of eighteenth-century slave life at the estate. Our illuminating conversations have expanded my horizons on this and other important subjects. Help from Linda L. Ayres and her assistant Dawn Bonner enabled me to use many of the visual images that complement and enhance the textual evidence. Dennis J. Pogue kindly made available findings of recent, extensive archaeological work, and he shared information about the evolution of the buildings and grounds. James C. Rees kindly offered encouragement, as he does with all scholarship related to the preservation and interpretation of the estate. Finally, my thanks go to the other staff members who extended gracious hospitality and assistance over the years.

Beyond the Potomac shore, in some cases far beyond it, is a group of scholars who are vital to my sense of intellectual community. The breadth of their vision, the joy they derive from scholarly pursuits, and the quality of their research have been my own joy to behold. With appreciation I mention Philander D. Chase, John M. Cooper Jr., Suzanne Desan, Rhys Isaac, Ann Smart Martin, Merrill D. Peterson, Bruce A. Ragsdale, David J. Sorkin, and my sons, Bradford J. Vivian and Daniel J. Vivian.

Also beyond the Potomac shore, learned institutions forwarded this work in significant ways. Credit in this regard is due especially to the David Library of the American Revolution and its former director David J. Fowler; the George Washington Masonic National Memorial Association; the Library of Congress; the *Papers of George Washington* editorial project at the University of Virginia; the Special Collections Library at the University of Virginia; the University of Wisconsin–Madison libraries; the Virginia Foundation for the Humanities and Public Policy and its staff member Roberta Culbertson; the Virginia Historical Society and the staff members Nelson D. Lankford, Paul A. Levengood, Frances S. Pollard, and Janet Schwarz; and the Wisconsin Historical Society. At the University of Wisconsin–Madison, the Graduate School and the Institute for Research in the Humanities generously provided financial support. Institutions that granted permission for reproduction of material from their collections, as well as several publishers who allowed inclusion of copyrighted material, are appropriately acknowledged in conjunction with the documents, illustrations, and maps.

From the day I approached Richard K. Holway at the University of Virginia Press about this project, he has enthusiastically supported it, and his thoughtful comments have improved the book. With insight and diligence, Ellen C. Hickman assisted in preparing the final manuscript for the Press. In seeing the book through to completion, I benefited from the expertise and care of Angie Hogan, Toni Mortimer, Hannah Nyala West, and Ellen Satrom.

Words alone cannot convey the extent to which my husband, Christopher, my children, Daniel, Bradford, and Deborah, and family members Jennifer and Anne have encouraged and forwarded my efforts. Suffice it to say that I am blessed.

EXPERIENCING MOUNT VERNON

INTRODUCTION

IN FEBRUARY 1784, shortly after returning home from the War for Independence, George Washington announced to Lafayette, "I am become a private citizen on the banks of the Potomac . . . retired from all public employments." At Mount Vernon he would "move gently down the stream of life, until I sleep with my Fathers." Yet, as a visitor noted the following year, Washington "did not by any means spend his time in idle repose, but . . . employed his talent in ways to make [his country] flourish."[1] At home he functioned in a cultural landscape largely of his own making, one filled with tangible memories of the American Revolution and one intentionally designed to further the nation's success.

At a time when neither public museums nor a national library yet existed in the United States, Washington had hauled home from the army his wartime papers, congressional medals honoring military and diplomatic achievements, his camp tent, and "trophies of American valor by sea and land." Flags captured in battle hung from downstairs walls, the voluminous papers resided in an upstairs room, and commemorative medals were brought out for visitors to admire. Over time other items enhanced this nationally important assemblage, among them prints of John Trumbull's scenes of the signing of the Declaration of Independence and of battlefield heroism, Houdon's famous life bust of Washington, and the first set of presidential china. For the hundreds of strangers and acquaintances who saw Mount Vernon each year in the 1780s and 1790s, these artifacts offered tangible connections to the winning of independence and Americans' experiments in creating representative governments.[2]

Moreover, George and Martha Washington functioned as living links to the Revolution. People wanted to see the general for themselves, to take the measure of the man. Having done so, they variously pronounced him "the first man in the world," "superior even to the Roman heroes themselves," and a "pure and virtuous champion" of Americans' rights. Martha Washington won praise for her congeniality and reminiscences, for being devoid of any "affectation of superiority," and for presenting visitors with mementos, cherished tokens of time spent at Mount Vernon. Those fortunate enough to be invited to dine and stay overnight might well find their host and hostess "delighting in anecdote and adventures." For example, Martha Washington recalled "what pleasure she took in the sound of the fifes and drums" as well as the "melancholy sight" of the army's disbanding, when "almost every soldier shed tears at parting with the General." Washington himself, typically reserved toward strangers, convivially swapped war stories with aging Continental veterans.[3]

Other authentic historical "characters" also inhabited the place. A slave named William Lee attracted attention because he had attended Washington throughout the war and even now seemed "always at his side." After a short stroll from the mansion to the stable, visitors encountered Washington's favorite warhorse, old Nelson, who had "carried the General almost always during the war," and a second steed, allegedly the finest in the Continental army. Standing before them, visitors imagined how these animals had "heard the roaring of many a cannon in their time."[4]

As a cultural landscape, therefore, Mount Vernon functioned as a place of remembrance and homage. More important from Washington's perspective was another element of this landscape: namely, he used his domestic setting to engage people in thinking about the future of the

United States and to disseminate his views on the subject. A Pole named Julian Niemcewicz caught the priorities one evening in 1798: he wanted Washington to reminisce about the war, but recognized that his host preferred the subject of agriculture, which he deemed vitally important to the nation's future. Other conversations ranged from the need for a stable national government, to the advantages of opening the North American interior to white settlement and trade, and, in the 1790s, to the threatening trajectory of the French Revolution. People were amazed at Washington's prodigious memory and detailed knowledge of the country. No one seemed "better informed regarding the present situation of the United States."[5]

In addition to conversing, sometimes passionately, about his hopes for the country, Washington devoted an enormous amount of time, thought, and labor (his own and his workers') to transforming the physical landscape at Mount Vernon into a model agricultural operation, one intended to inspire all Americans. Here is the most ambitious connection he forged between the estate and the American Revolution. He fervently wanted Mount Vernon's fields and the mansion grounds to model order, efficiency, industriousness, and agricultural prosperity. For he strongly believed, in keeping with many contemporaries, that the success, indeed the very survival of the Republic would depend on the self-discipline and self-sufficiency that conscientious husbandry fostered.

Strongly influenced by English agricultural reformers, Washington replaced traditional tobacco production with grains; experimented with over sixty crops; instituted deep plowing, fertilizing, and crop rotation; and, to enclose his fields, ordered that hundreds of shrubs be planted as live "fences." "Every improvement in husbandry should be gratefully received and peculiarly fostered in this Country," he opined, because good farming advanced "our respectability in a national point of view." Under Washington's watchful eye, and through copious correspondence with hired farm managers during the years of his presidency, Mount Vernon, with its "Good fences, clear grounds, and extensive cultivation," seemed "something uncommon in this part of the World." These improvements—and the vision that inspired them—died with Washington.[6]

Upon his death in 1799 Martha Washington inherited a life interest in the property, some eight thousand acres, and she continued living there until her death in May 1802. Because the couple had not produced any children during their long marriage, the estate descended to a succession of collateral Washington kin. The largest share went to Bushrod Washington, a nephew and Supreme Court justice, whose legacy included the mansion, family tomb, and four thousand acres. He and his wife, Julia Ann Blackburn Washington, made Mount Vernon their home until their deaths within days of each other in 1829. They, too, died childless, and 1,225 of Bushrod's acreage, including the mansion and tomb, went to his nephew, a man named John Augustine Washington. The new proprietor quickly succumbed to ill health and died in 1832, whereupon his wife, Jane Charlotte Blackburn Washington, succeeded him as owner. Finally, at her death in 1855, her eldest son, also named John Augustine Washington, inherited the place; he lived there until relinquishing possession to the Mount Vernon Ladies' Association in 1860. To summarize, therefore, from the beginning of the nineteenth century to 1860, when Mount Vernon passed out of the family, the estate (meaning the mansion, family burial grounds, and varying amounts of adjacent acreage), had only five owners.[7]

In contrast, the number of visitors was enormous. Whereas hundreds of people annually traveled to Mount Vernon after the War for Independence, during the nineteenth century the numbers swelled into the thousands. By the 1850s an estimated ten thousand men, women, and children flocked to the site each year—even as it remained the private residence and working plantation of Washington family members. It was

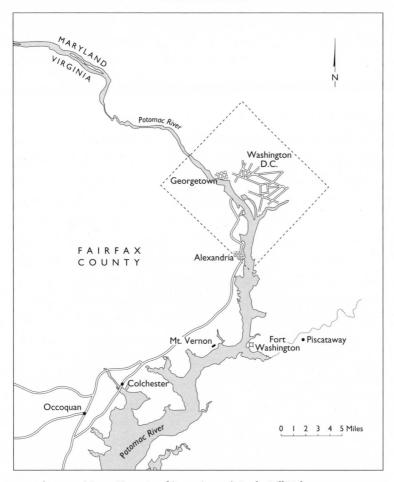

Mount Vernon and its environs. (Map by Bill Nelson,
adapted from Herman Böÿe's *A Map of the State of Virginia*, 1825)

said that most everyone who visited the new nation's capital city also
made the fifteen-mile trek to Mount Vernon. Until regular steamboat
service was established in the 1850s, the majority traveled overland,
through Alexandria and over a rutted road that crossed the wooded ter-

rain of northern Virginia and brought them to the estate. Passing between two gatehouses where an elderly African American typically met them, visitors entered the grounds and first saw, on a rise about three-fourths of a mile to the east, the mansion.

Whether ordinary citizens or presidents and congressmen, aging Revolutionary War veterans or schoolchildren, kin or foreign dignitaries—all came as pilgrims to the site that, in the public imagination, had become the nation's most sacred place. People spoke of being on "solemn pilgrimage" to their "Mecca," "the most hallowed spot in America's soul." Here they walked over grounds consecrated "in the holiest manner" by the country's "political saviour." Here they imaginatively touched and affirmed the greatness not only of Washington but of the entire Revolutionary heritage. Here, too, pilgrims held onto America's heroic age even as it receded into the past. These things they did while touring the mansion, touching the pistols and sword Washington had carried into battle, strolling over ground that had received his footsteps, marveling at trees and plants once nurtured by his hand, weeping before the tomb, and, typically, carrying away some memento of the experience.[8]

Such rituals, worked out through interactions among visitors and the resident Washingtons over half a century, served important civic purposes. What better place for the old to reaffirm and the young to learn about the nation's founding principles and greatest achievements? What better place to honor Washington and aspire to emulate his virtues? Moreover, in a sprawling young republic increasingly rived by sectional conflict, experiencing Mount Vernon as hallowed ground, so intimately associated with the country's heroic origins, inevitably fostered "national feelings."[9]

In fact, during the decade before the Civil War, as one sectional crisis after another tore at the body politic, some visitors passionately, publicly, urged even more Americans to come and personally experience Mount

Vernon. Walking its pathways, standing before the tomb, venerating the man who "knew no Mason & Dixon's line" but, rather, "embraced the whole country"—these ritual acts might quell the forces of disunion, or so it was argued. When those forces would not be quelled, however, both the Union and Confederate armies accorded the property remarkable status: for nearly the entire Civil War, only Mount Vernon stood as continuous neutral ground between the combatants.[10]

Copious and rich evidence offers access to the entwined worlds of the Washingtons and the tens of thousands of people who saw Mount Vernon between the end of the Revolutionary War and the end of the Civil War. Well over one hundred eyewitness accounts are preserved in visitors' private correspondence and journals, newspaper and magazine articles, and public addresses. For the Washington owners, from George and Martha to the younger John Augustine, letters, diaries, and plantation records reveal the challenges they routinely faced in trying simultaneously to maintain some semblance of domestic privacy, farm the land with enslaved and free laborers, and contend with the crush of visitors. This volume gathers together thirty-eight accounts written by individuals who visited Mount Vernon between 1785 and 1865. In addition, a few documents from the succession of Washington owners span four generations and are included here so that family voices, too, might be heard. The last of the private owners, John Augustine Washington, sold the mansion and adjacent acreage to the Mount Vernon Ladies' Association (founded 1853), which took possession in 1860. Glimpses of its early organizing activities and of life at the estate during the Civil War add yet another dimension to the documentary evidence.

Historic artifacts, visual images, and maps are just as informative, in their own ways, as the texts. All of these sources, plus the eighteenth-century buildings and landscape design, make Mount Vernon perhaps the best documented of all southern plantations. In these pages, therefore, contemporary paintings, sketches, and early photographic images and maps complement the texts and, in turn, are complemented by the words. Modern photographs are reproduced here only when contemporary images were not available.

The documents begin with the 1784 letter to Lafayette in which George Washington affirmed his intent to live out his days in pastoral retirement. They end with the manuscript journal of George W. Clymans, a Union soldier and veteran of Sherman's march to the sea. Clymans's brief sojourn at Mount Vernon occurred in May 1865, the month after the South surrendered and Abraham Lincoln was assassinated and shortly before a triumphal two-day parade of the Union army in Washington, D.C. Over the eight decades between letter and journal, the documentary record discloses a variety of experiences at this one place. Reverential behavior dominated, but not exclusively so. Many visitors felt awe-struck, others disappointed. Washington family members' reactions to them ranged from dutiful acceptance to unfeigned annoyance. The family also received both commendation and condemnation for its management of the property. Ideas about what should become of Mount Vernon varied, notwithstanding consensus that public access must be permitted. One place, and diverse reactions to it.

Beyond the texts' descriptive passages, beyond the expressions of deep emotion, the eyewitness testimony adds importantly to a vital area of scholarship: inquiry into the creation and shaping of the memory, and therefore the meaning, of the American Revolution. Members of the founding generation commonly believed that their Revolution promised to change the course of human history. "Posterity are virtually involved in the contest," argued Thomas Paine in *Common Sense* (1776), "and will be more or less affected to the end of time." Half a century later Thomas Jefferson was more explicit. In the last letter he wrote, just ten days before his death on 4 July 1826, he voiced hope that the Declaration of

Independence, the nation's premier incantation to human liberty, would forever "be to the world, what I believe it will be, (to some parts sooner, to others later, but finally to all,) the signal . . . to assume the blessings and security of self-government."[11]

The Revolution, therefore, had to be remembered, and it was—in public celebrations of the Fourth of July, anniversaries of important battles, and Washington's birthday; in reminiscences that women and men of the founding generation passed on to their children and grandchildren; and in funeral orations for war veterans and statesmen. As Americans remembered in these and other ways, they also fashioned a grand, aphoristic narrative of heroic national origins, a narrative that reduced the Revolution's causes to British oppression, extolled liberty and self-government, and pledged that future generations would never forget this signal moment in human affairs. That narrative, with all the symbols and rituals associated with it, became a template of national identity.[12]

In the pantheon of heroes (and a few heroines) who inhabited the Revolutionary narrative, uncontested preeminence went to George Washington. Even during his lifetime he was idealized as "the perfect" citizen, possessed of "all the virtues" required for the nation's success. In repeatedly placing the public good ahead of self-interest, he exemplified this cardinal principle of Revolutionary ideology. Nineteenth-century Americans stood in awe of him, not only for what he had accomplished in his military and political careers but, equally important, because he had so readily relinquished power and returned, Cincinnatus-like, to the plow, to "the rural field, the solitary shades of Vernon." Hence, in the oft-repeated words of Henry "Light Horse Harry" Lee, Washington stood "first in war, first in peace, and first in the hearts of his countrymen."[13]

The historian Hannah Arendt once remarked that people's conceptions of reality depend not only on those "who have seen and heard and will remember" events and ideas but also on "the transformation of the intangible into the tangibility of things." Mount Vernon, the most tangible link to Washington and his "departed greatness," performed this transformative function for countless nineteenth-century Americans. Indeed, just as they considered him a "spotless" paragon of virtue, they imagined his home and burial ground as the repository, even guardian, of the highest ideals of the Revolution. However much the nation at large teemed with change, rampant individualism, acquisitiveness, and contention, Mount Vernon bespoke sacrifice for the public good and selfless courage. Here people remembered and paid homage to the past, while also rededicating themselves to all that Washington and the Revolution had come to represent. Here they contemplated what the nation, at its best, might be. Mount Vernon was both relic and inspiration.[14]

Such was the site's hold on the public imagination. No wonder, then, that as the nineteenth century progressed, people laid claim, with increasing stridency, to the property, the "common ground of every American citizen." In 1840 Jane Charlotte Washington, the actual owner, acknowledged that "the Nation . . . shares [Mount Vernon] with us." What made "the endless intrusions, and sacrifice of every thing like private right and domestic privacy" worthwhile, she believed, were the nationalistic sentiments and loyalty fostered in individuals who visited, and thereby experienced, the place.[15]

Yet no matter what the Washingtons sacrificed because of their understanding of the public good and no matter how much people accorded the site stunning instrumentality as a repository of historical memory and Revolutionary idealism, the hallowed ground also became contested ground. One point of major contention concerned the eventual fate of Mount Vernon. Even as family members struggled to preserve the mansion area much as their illustrious forebear had left it, others variously advocated using it as a summer retreat for the incumbent American president, an asylum for "worn out and mutilated" veterans, or, faintly echoing Washington's eighteenth-century vision, an agricultural school that would encourage improved farming practices. These and other proposals implied or openly advocated some kind of public ownership. Dialogue about the possibilities lasted for decades and, as became clear only in retrospect, laid the foundations of the historic preservation movement in the United States.[16]

In their entirety, the materials presented in this volume offer compelling evidence that the countless Americans who traveled to Mount Vernon between the 1780s and the 1850s, as well as the resident Washingtons who accommodated them, paved the way for the Mount Vernon Ladies' Association. Beginning with George and Martha Washington's efforts to make their estate nationally meaningful, the family and the visiting throngs created the rituals enacted there, and they urged that, somehow, the nation's most sacred place must be preserved for future generations. The association built on this solid foundation, beginning in 1853.

A second major point of contention over the site concerned slavery. As a plantation populated by enslaved African Americans, the national Mecca could not be immune to this most divisive sectional issue. Slaves not only cared for the Washington family and worked the fields, they routinely ushered pilgrims around the site. To the acute consternation of the Washingtons, abolitionists sometimes spread their views among Mount Vernon slaves (witness Bushrod Washington's dramatic reaction to the best-documented episode of this kind, which is included in this volume). Furthermore, long censure of the Washingtons as slave owners climaxed in the 1850s when critics insisted that this place—where people honored the man credited, above all others, with creating the first nation explicitly founded on principles of human liberty—must be cleansed of human bondage.[17]

A combination of factors led John Augustine Washington to relinquish possession, on George Washington's birthday in 1860, of the property's core acreage to the Mount Vernon Ladies' Association of the Union, as the organization is officially named. Beginning in the late 1840s John Augustine and his mother, Jane Charlotte Washington, had expressed willingness to sell the mansion and some of the land to the federal government. It soon became clear, however, that the state of Virginia would block such a sale by exercising its right, under the United States Constitution, to prevent transfer of property within its borders to the national government. John Augustine Washington then opened what proved to be protracted negotiations with the state, but he was unable to effect a sale.[18]

Advent of the Mount Vernon Ladies' Association therefore promised to break the political deadlock, and to relieve John Augustine and his wife and children of the burdens they bore as residents of what, in effect, had long since become a national historic site. Women, legally barred from voting and political office, would rescue the hallowed ground on behalf of the American people. Well before John Augustine Washington consented to this development, for which there was no precedent in the United States, a South Carolinian named Ann Pamela Cunningham organized the association and became its guiding force. Not content to sit quietly until Washington decided what to do, Cunningham enlisted the aid, first, of southern women and then of women throughout the country. They promptly organized local and state chapters, publicized the association's salvific intent, gained advice and support from influential men, and began raising money. Once Washington's negotiations with the state of Virginia collapsed, he agreed in 1858 to sell two hundred acres to the association, with the provisos that the Washington family would retain control of the tombs and burial ground and, second, that the property would revert to the family if the association ceased to exist.[19]

It is vivid testament to the public veneration of George Washington that the association easily and swiftly raised the asking price of two hundred thousand dollars plus additional money for restoration and operating expenses. And this occurred despite a severe economic depression in the late 1850s. Meanwhile, John Augustine Washington retained 1,025 acres of his original inheritance, which continued to be worked with hired and slave labor, but he and his family relocated to Fauquier County, Virginia. The association eventually purchased some three hundred additional acres of Mount Vernon land, thereby bringing its total holdings to about five hundred acres.

Outbreak of the Civil War in the spring of 1861 halted the association's momentum. Ann Pamela Cunningham returned to South Carolina, leaving behind a New York woman named Sarah Tracy, the only association member who lived on the property during the war, along with an estate manager and a few African Americans whom she paid for their services. Union and Confederate forces constantly operated nearby, and to Tracy largely belongs credit for getting both sides to agree not to occupy the estate. As for individual soldiers, they visited in droves, as had so many Americans before them. In the words of George W. Clymans, the Pennsylvania soldier whose 1865 journal entry closes this volume, "we feel awed into silence."[20]

Notes

1. George Washington to Lafayette, 1 Feb. 1784, in *The Papers of George Washington: Confederation Series*, ed. W. W. Abbot et al., 6 vols. (Charlottesville, Va., 1992–97), 1:87–88; Luigi Castiglioni, *Luigi Castiglioni's Viaggio: Travels in the United States of North America, 1785–1787*, trans. and ed. Antonio Pace (Syracuse, N.Y., 1983), 113.

2. Robert Hunter, *Quebec to Carolina in 1785–1786: Being the Travel Diary and Observations of Robert Hunter, Jr., a Young Merchant of London*, ed. Louis B. Wright and Marion Tinling (San Marino, Calif., 1943), 192–93, 196; Julian Ursyn Niemcewicz, *Under Their Vine and Fig Tree: Travels through America in 1797–1799, 1805 . . .*, trans. and ed. Metchie J. E. Budka (Elizabeth, N.J., 1965), 96–97, 104–5. The

quotation is from Joshua Brookes, "A Dinner at Mount Vernon: From the Unpub-lished Journal of Joshua Brookes (1773-1859)," ed. R. W. G. Vail, *New York Historical Society Quarterly* 31 (1947): 78. On Washington's management of his papers, see W. W. Abbot, "An Uncommon Awareness of Self: The Papers of George Washington," *Prologue: Quarterly Journal of the National Archives and Records Administration* 21 (1989): 7-19.

3. Hunter, *Quebec to Carolina in 1785-1786*, 192-94, 196-97; Elkanah Watson, *Men and Times of the Revolution; or, Memoirs of Elkanah Watson, Including Journals of Travels in Europe and America, from 1777 to 1842, with His Correspondence with Public Men and Reminiscences and Incidents of the Revolution*, ed. Winslow C. Watson (New York, 1856), 244; J. P. Brissot de Warville, *New Travels in the United States of America, 1788*, trans. and ed. Mara S. Vamos and Durand Echeverria (Cambridge, Mass., 1964), 343; Benjamin Henry Latrobe, *The Virginia Journals of Benjamin Henry Latrobe, 1795-1798*, ed. Edward C. Carter II et al., 2 vols. (New Haven, Conn., 1977), 1:168; Niemcewicz, *Under Their Vine and Fig Tree*, 104; Elizabeth Ambler Carrington to Anne Fisher, 22 and 27 Nov. 1799, in "A Visit to Mount Vernon—A Letter of Mrs. Edward Carrington to Her Sister, Mrs. George Fisher," *William and Mary Quarterly*, 2nd ser., 18 (1938): 202.

4. Watson, *Men and Times of the Revolution*, 244; Hunter, *Quebec to Carolina in 1785-1786*, 196.

5. Niemcewicz, *Under Their Vine and Fig Tree*, 102, 107; Watson, *Men and Times of the Revolution*, 244-46; Hunter, *Quebec to Carolina in 1785-1786*, 193; Olney Winsor to Hope Winsor, 31 Mar. 1788, Miscellaneous Manuscripts Collection, Rhode Island Historical Society, Providence; Brissot de Warville, *New Travels in the United States of America, 1788*, 344; Castiglioni, *Luigi Castiglioni's Viaggio*, 113. A particu-larly useful approach to the study of cultural landscapes is D. W. Meinig, "The Beholding Eye: Ten Versions of the Same Scene," in *The Interpretation of Ordinary Landscapes: Geographical Essays* (New York: Oxford University Press, 1979), 33-48.

6. Jean B. Lee explores this subject in "Mount Vernon Plantation: A Model for the Republic," in *Slavery at the Home of George Washington*, ed. Philip J. Schwarz (Mount Vernon, Va.: Mount Vernon Ladies' Association, 2001), 12-45. The quotations are from GW to Samuel Chamberline, 3 Apr. 1788, *Papers of George Washington: Confederation Series* 6:190, and Latrobe, *Virginia Journals of Benjamin Henry Latrobe, 1795-1798* 1:162-63, 165.

7. Will of G. Washington [9 July 1799], in *The Papers of George Washington: Retirement Series*, ed. W. W. Abbot et al., 4 vols. (Charlottesville, Va., 1998-99), 4:477-80, 487-88; will of Bushrod Washington, 10 July 1826, in *Wills of George*

Washington and His Immediate Ancestors, ed. Worthington C. Ford (Brooklyn, N.Y., 1891), 151, 153; will of John Augustine Washington, 6 Aug. 1822, copy at MVLA; will of Jane Charlotte Washington, 3 Oct. 1854, in *The Washingtons and Their Homes,* by John W. Wayland (Staunton, Va.: McClure Printing Co., 1944), 227; "A Visit to Mount Vernon," *New York Times,* 10 Mar. 1860. Jane Charlotte Washington was a niece of Julia Ann Blackburn Washington. For the boundaries of Mount Vernon as of 1793, see GW's survey (see the map on p. 35). For John Augustine Washington's map of his Mount Vernon lands in 1831, see the map on p. 133.

The remaining four thousand acres of the estate—that is, the land that did not descend to Bushrod Washington and his heirs—was divided among other Washington kin. Lawrence Lewis (son of GW's deceased sister Betsy), along with his wife, Eleanor Parke Custis (Martha Washington's granddaughter), received the tract subsequently named Woodlawn. Other tracts went to sons of GW's deceased nephew and farm manager, George Augustine Washington. George Washington Parke Custis, who along with his sister Eleanor was raised at Mount Vernon, did not receive any land there; rather, GW bequeathed him some twelve hundred acres west of Alexandria, where Custis built Arlington. Will of G. Washington [9 July 1799], *Papers of George Washington: Retirement Series* 4:488–89.

8. This and subsequent paragraphs incorporate perspectives offered in Jean B. Lee, "Historical Memory, Sectional Strife, and the American Mecca: Mount Vernon, 1783–1853," *Virginia Magazine of History and Biography* 109 (2001): 255–300. Quotations are from the following sources, in the order in which they appear in the paragraph: "Visit to the Tomb of Washington," *National Intelligencer* (Washington, D.C.), 24 Feb. 1818; T. L. Forrest to the editors of the *Chicago Journal,* 27 June 1851, MVLA; L. Osgood, "Visit to Mount Vernon, 1839," MVLA; "Communication," *National Intelligencer,* 24 May 1827; *Poulson's American Daily Advertiser* (Philadelphia), 20 Oct. 1818.

9. Quotation in *Poulson's American Daily Advertiser,* 20 Oct. 1818.

10. Quotation in "The 'Seventh' at Home. Full Account of the Visit to Washington. . . . Description of Mount Vernon," *New York Herald* (New York City), 12 July 1858. On Mount Vernon as neutral ground during the Civil War, see Gerald W. Johnson, *Mount Vernon: The Story of a Shrine,* rev. ed. (Mount Vernon, Va.: Mount Vernon Ladies' Association, 1991), 34–35.

11. Thomas Paine, *Common Sense,* ed. Isaac Kramnick (New York: Penguin Books, 1976), 82; Thomas Jefferson to Roger C. Weightman, 24 June 1826, in *Thomas Jefferson, Writings,* ed. Merrill D. Peterson (New York, 1984), 1517.

12. Extended discussion of the interpretation advanced in this paragraph is in Jean

B. Lee, "Touchstone of American Identities: Memory and the Revolution, 1775–1825," in *Rhetoric, Independence, and Nationhood,* ed. Stephen E. Lucas, vol. 2 of *A Rhetorical History of the United States,* 10 vols. (East Lansing: Michigan State University Press, forthcoming). For other perspectives consult Merrill D. Peterson, *The Jefferson Image in the American Mind* (New York: Oxford University Press, 1960, 1985); Michael Kammen, *A Season of Youth: The American Revolution and the Historical Imagination* (New York: Oxford University Press, 1978); David Lowenthal, *The Past Is a Foreign Country* (New York: Cambridge University Press, 1985), 105–24; Michael Kammen, *Mystic Chords of Memory: The Transformation of Tradition in American Culture* (New York: Alfred A. Knopf, 1991); David Hackett Fischer, *Paul Revere's Ride* (New York: Oxford University Press, 1994); Lorett Treese, *Valley Forge: Making and Remaking a National Symbol* (University Park: Pennsylvania State University Press, 1995); David Waldstreicher, *In the Midst of Perpetual Fetes: The Making of American Nationalism, 1776–1820* (Chapel Hill: University of North Carolina Press, for the Institute of Early American History and Culture, 1997); Robert E. McGlone, "Deciphering Memory: John Adams and the Authorship of the Declaration of Independence," *Journal of American History* 85 (1998): 411–38; Sarah J. Purcell, *Sealed with Blood: War, Sacrifice, and Memory in Revolutionary America* (Philadelphia: University of Pennsylvania Press, 2002); Elizabeth M. Covart, "Live Free or Die: A Generation Remembers the Battle of Bunker Hill" (senior honors thesis, Pennsylvania State University, 2003); David Hackett Fischer, *Washington's Crossing* (New York: Oxford University Press, 2004).

13. Brissot de Warville, *New Travels in the United States of America, 1788,* 345; M. R. Nowland, extract of a visit to Mount Vernon, 12 Nov. 1820, MVLA. Henry Lee's phrase is in his eulogy to GW, delivered to the United States Congress and printed in *The Washingtoniana: Containing a Sketch of the Life and Death of the Late Gen. George Washington; With a Collection of Elegant Eulogies, Orations, Poems, &c. . . .* (Lancaster, Pa., 1802), 34. On the apotheosis of GW, see Robert P. Hay, "George Washington: American Moses," *American Quarterly* 21 (1969): 780–91; Marcus Cunliffe, *George Washington: Man and Monument* (Boston: Little, Brown, 1958); Garry Wills, *Cincinnatus: George Washington and the Enlightenment* (New York: Doubleday, 1984); Barry Schwartz, *George Washington: The Making of an American Symbol* (New York: Free Press, 1987). On the importance of the concept of the public good, see Gordon S. Wood, *The Creation of the American Republic, 1776–1787* (Chapel Hill: University of North Carolina Press, for the Institute of Early American History and Culture, 1969), 53–65.

14. Hannah Arendt, *The Human Condition* (Chicago: University of Chicago Press, 1958), 95; Nowland, extract of a visit to Mount Vernon; Cunliffe, *George Washington: Man and Monument,* 21; Lee, "Historical Memory, Sectional Strife, and the American Mecca," 264, 295–97.

15. "The 'Seventh' at Home"; J. C. Washington to George Corbin Washington, 25 May 1840, MVLA.

16. "Mount Vernon and the Monument," *Daily National Intelligencer* (Washington, D.C.), 3 May 1848; "Mount Vernon," ibid., 28 June 1853; "Petition of Citizens of Philad[elphi]a in favor of the purchase of Mount Vernon and the establishment of an agricultural school at that place," 1849, in papers of the 30th Congress, 2nd Session, Senate, Committee on Military Affairs, at the National Archives and Records Administration, Washington, D.C. Lee analyzes the protracted discourse over what should become of Mount Vernon in "Historical Memory, Sectional Strife, and the American Mecca," 278, 281, 287–93.

17. GW's slave censuses dated 1786 (see "1786: Laboring Hands," below) and 1799 list, respectively, 216 and 319 bondpeople. The slaves he owned outright were manumitted through his will, whereas those belonging to the estate of Martha Washington's first husband, Daniel Parke Custis, descended to Custis heirs when she died. The nineteenth-century estate owners maintained their own slaves at the plantation, in numbers ranging from thirty to one hundred. Slave census, 18 Feb. 1786, in *The Diaries of George Washington,* ed. Donald Jackson and Dorothy Twohig, 6 vols. (Charlottesville, Va., 1976–79), 4:277–83; slave census, ca. June 1799, *Papers of George Washington: Retirement Series* 4:527–42; B. Washington, "List of My Negroes," 24 July 1815, in Mount Vernon Farm Book [1814–45], fols. 35–36, MVLA; Lynn C. McMillion and Jane K. Wall, comps., *Fairfax County, Virginia: 1820 Federal Population Census and Census of Manufacturers* (Vienna, Va.: McMillion, 1976), 24; John A. Washington, "List of Negroes," 10 Mar. 1850, John Augustine Washington Farm Book, 1850–52, MVLA.

18. Jean B. Lee, "Jane C. Washington, Family, and Nation at Mount Vernon, 1830–55," in *Women Shaping the South: Creating and Confronting Change,* ed. Angela Boswell and Judith McArthur (Columbia: University of Missouri Press, 2005).

19. This and the next paragraph draw on the editor's unpublished research and on Johnson, *Mount Vernon,* chap. 1.

20. George W. Clymans, "1865: 'We Believe the Place Where We are Standing to Be Holy,'" below; Dorothy Troth Muir, ed., *Mount Vernon: The Civil War Years* (Mount Vernon, Va.: Mount Vernon Ladies' Association, 1993).

General George Washington, a portrait by Rembrandt Peale, 1823, based on a life study. (Courtesy of the Mount Vernon Ladies' Association)

1784

"A Private Citizen on the Banks of the Potomac"
George Washington

Washington's resignation from the Continental army and his return to Mount Vernon in December 1783 were highly symbolic acts. In this letter to Lafayette, dated 1 February 1784, he affirmed what he had already announced publicly: after retiring to private life he would seek no further public office—and the power that went with it. Thus he rejected the path that, historically, many other military leaders had taken toward autocratic rule. Only when Washington feared that American self-government was in jeopardy did he agree to alter his "march," from retirement to service in the Constitutional Convention of 1787. Still, his retirement to Mount Vernon after the War for Independence, and again at the conclusion of his presidency in 1797, evoked awe among Americans and contributed to Washington's heroic image.

Here Washington writes to Lafayette in a tone that bespeaks the closeness of their relationship. A few months later Lafayette visited Mount Vernon, and when the two men parted, they rightly believed it to be their last farewell.

This letter appears in *The Papers of George Washington: Confederation Series*, edited by W. W. Abbot et al., 6 vols. (Charlottesville, Va., 1992–97), 1:87–88, and is reprinted with permission of the University of Virginia Press.

At length my Dear Marquis I am become a private citizen on the banks of the Potomac, & under the shadow of my own Vine & my own Fig tree, free from the bustle of a camp & the busy scenes of public life, I am solacing myself with those tranquil enjoyments, of which the Soldier who is ever in pursuit of fame—the Statesman whose watchful days & sleepless Nights are spent in devising schemes to promote the welfare of his own—perhaps the ruin of other countries, as if this Globe was insufficient for us all—& the Courtier who is always watching the countenance of his Prince, in hopes of catching a gracious smile, can have very little conception. I am not only retired from all public employments, but I am retireing within myself; & shall be able to view the solitary walk, & tread the paths of private life with heartfelt satisfaction—Envious of none, I am determined to be pleased with all. & this my dear friend, being the order for my march, I will move gently down the stream of life, until I sleep with my Fathers.

1785

"Two of the Richest Days of My Life"
Elkanah Watson

Among founders of the new nation, Washington possessed one of the most expansive visions of its potential. Having served during the 1750s both as a surveyor of Virginia's western lands and an officer in the Seven Years' War, he knew the vast American interior firsthand. As commander of the Continental army during the War for Independence, he personally became acquainted with the original states from Maryland to New England and also gained much knowledge of those lying south of Virginia. These experiences served him well during the 1780s when, at Mount Vernon, he contemplated and advocated the nation's development.

In his imaginings, the Potomac River valley played a central role: because its headwaters nearly reached those of the Ohio River system, if the entire length of the Potomac could be made navigable, that would open the interior of the continent to people and trade—and also foster political ties between the original states and the backcountry.

During two days spent at Mount Vernon, Elkanah Watson, a well-traveled New Englander, found Washington intently focused on how these goals might be accomplished. Therefore the guest personally witnessed the way his host used his domestic setting to promote American nationalism. Like other visitors, Watson also expressed fascination not only with the retired general's preferred topics of conversation but also his appearance, mannerisms, and daily routines.

Shortly after Watson's visit, Washington hosted what became known as the Mount Vernon Conference, at which delegates from Virginia and Maryland discussed jurisdictional matters concerning the river. The recent formation of the Potomac Company, of which Washington served as president, prompted the meeting. The company undertook the first major internal improvement project in the United States: making the river navigable from its falls at Georgetown, Maryland, to its headwaters in the Appalachian Mountains.

This account is in *Men and Times of the Revolution; or, Memoirs of Elkanah Watson, Including Journals of Travels in Europe and America, from 1777 to 1842, with His Correspondence with Public Men and Reminiscences and Incidents of the Revolution*, edited by Winslow C. Watson (New York, 1856), 243–46.

I had feasted my imagination for several days in the near prospect of a visit to Mount Vernon, the seat of Washington. No pilgrim ever approached Mecca with deeper enthusiasm. I arrived there in the afternoon of January 23d, '85. I was the bearer of the letter from Gen[eral]

Green, with another from Col. Fitzgerald, one of the former aids of Washington.[1] . . . Although assured that these credentials would secure me a respectful reception, I trembled with awe as I came into the presence of this great man. I found him at table with Mrs. Washington and his private family, and was received in the native dignity and with that urbanity so peculiarly combined in the character of a soldier and eminent private gentleman. He soon put me at ease, by unbending, in a free and affable conversation.

The cautious reserve, which wisdom and policy dictated, whilst engaged in rearing the glorious fabric of our independence, was evidently the result of consummate prudence, and not characteristic of his nature. Although I had frequently seen him in the progress of the Revolution, and had corresponded with him from France in '81 and '82, this was the first occasion on which I had contemplated him in his private relations. I observed a peculiarity in his smile, which seemed to illuminate his eye; his whole countenance beamed with intelligence, while it commanded confidence and respect. The gentleman who had accompanied me from Alexandria, left in the evening, and I remained alone in the enjoyment of the society of Washington, for two of the richest days of my life. I saw him reaping the reward of his illustrious deeds, in the quiet shade of his beloved retirement. He was at the matured age of fifty-three. Alexander and Cæsar both died before they reached that period of life, and both had immortalized their names. How much stronger and nobler the claims of Washington to immortality! In the impulses of mad and selfish ambition, they acquired fame by wading to the conquest of the world through seas of blood. Washington, on the contrary, was parsimonious of the blood of his countrymen, and stood forth, the pure and virtuous champion of their rights, and formed for them, (not himself,) a mighty Empire.

To have communed with such a man in the bosom of his family, I shall always regard as one of the highest privileges, and most cherished incidents of my life. I found him kind and benignant in the domestic circle, revered and beloved by all around him; agreeably social, without ostentation; delighting in anecdote and adventures, without assumption; his domestic arrangements harmonious and systematic. His servants [slaves] seemed to watch his eye, and to anticipate his every wish; hence a look was equivalent to a command. His servant Billy,[2] the faithful companion of his military career, was always at his side. Smiling content animated and beamed on every countenance in his presence.

The first evening I spent under the wing of his hospitality, we sat a full hour at table by ourselves, without the least interruption, after the family had retired. I was extremely oppressed by a severe cold and excessive coughing, contracted by the exposure of a harsh winter journey. He pressed me to use some remedies, but I declined doing so. As usual after retiring, my coughing increased. When some time had elapsed, the door of my room was gently opened, and on drawing my bed-curtains, to my utter astonishment, I beheld Washington himself, standing at my bedside, with a bowl of hot tea in his hand. I was mortified and distressed beyond expression. This little incident, occurring in common life with an ordinary man, would not have been noticed; but as a trait of the benevolence and private virtue of Washington, deserves to be recorded.

He modestly waived all allusions to the events, in which he had acted so glorious and conspicuous a part. Much of his conversation had reference to the interior country, and to the opening of the navigation of the Potomac, by canals and locks, at the Seneca, the Great and Little Falls. His mind appeared to be deeply absorbed by that object, then in earnest contemplation. . . .

To demonstrate the practicability and the policy of diverting the trade of the immense interior world yet unexplored to the Atlantic cities, especially in view of the idea that the Mississippi would be opened by Spain,[3]

Benjamin Henry Latrobe's "View to the North from the Lawn at Mount Vernon," sketched during his visit to the estate in 1796, depicts, on the left side of the Potomac River, Washington's land extending to the horizon. To the right is the Maryland shore. At Mount Vernon, Washington imagined the Potomac as a gateway to the interior of the continent. (Courtesy of the Maryland Historical Society, Baltimore)

was his constant and favorite theme. To elucidate also the probability that the Detroit fur trade would take this direction, he produced to me the following estimates, which I copied, in his presence and with his aid, from the original manuscript:

From Detroit, at the head of Lake Erie, via Fort Pitt, (now Pittsburgh,) and Fort Cumberland, to the head of the

Potomac, is	607 miles.
To Richmond,	840 "
" Philadelphia,	741 "
" Albany,	943 "
" Montreal,	955 "

Thus it appeared that Alexandria is 348 miles nearer Detroit than Montreal, with only two carrying places[4] of about forty miles.

Since my travels in 1779, I had been deeply and constantly impressed with the importance of constructing canals to connect the various waters of America. This conviction was confirmed by the examination of numerous canals in Europe, and travelling extensively on several of them. Hearing little else for two days from the persuasive tongue of this great man, I confess completely infected me with the canal mania, and enkindled all my enthusiasm.

Washington pressed me earnestly to settle on the banks of the Potomac. At his suggestion I proceeded up the southern shore of the river, twenty-two miles from Alexandria, to examine the proposed route of the canal.

1. Nathanael Greene, one of GW's most talented and trusted generals during the war; Colonel John Fitzgerald, merchant of Alexandria.

2. William Lee.

3. The Spanish empire in North America, extending from Florida to California, straddled the lower Mississippi River valley. Although allied with the United States in the War for Independence, Spanish leaders did not want to see rapid population growth and economic development in the lands that Great Britain ceded to the new nation in the 1783 peace treaty. These lands lay between the Appalachian Mountains and the Mississippi, and already people from the original thirteen states were pressing westward into the Ohio country and Kentucky. In an attempt, therefore, to protect its northern borderlands, Spain in 1784 blocked access to the lower reaches of the river, to the detriment of American commerce. GW clearly hoped that the Spanish would relent.

4. Portages.

1785

"THE FIRST MAN IN THE WORLD"
Robert Hunter

By the time Robert Hunter, a young Scotsman, visited Mount Vernon in November 1785, Washington had embarked on an ambitious effort to transform his estate into a model for the entire nation. He wanted to inspire Americans to adopt more efficient agricultural and labor practices, and he also was intent on improving the estate aesthetically. These were not trivial matters, considering the powerful ideology of the American Revolution, which deemed self-governing republics the most fragile form of government. Their survival depended, it was commonly believed, on an industrious, well ordered, and virtuous citizenry, which well-practiced husbandry was thought to promote. An improved Mount Vernon, therefore, was integral to Washington's vision of what the United States might become.

Hunter observed the estate in the process of transformation. At the same time, he eagerly sought out information about and reminders of the recent war. His description of Martha Washington shows her fully engaged in conversation with visitors.

This visitor's description is found in *Quebec to Carolina in 1785–1786: Being the Travel Diary and Observations of Robert Hunter, Jr., a Young Merchant of London,* edited by Louis B. Wright and Marion Tinling (San Marino, Calif., 1943), 191–98, and is reprinted with permission of the Henry E. Huntington Library.

After breakfast I waited on Colonel Fitzgerald.[1] . . . [A]t half past eleven we left Alexandria with Mr. Lee,[2] the president of Congress, his son, and the servants. You have a fine view of the Potomac, till you enter a wood. A small rivulet here divides the General's estate from the neighboring farmer's. His seat breaks out beautifully upon you when you little expect, being situated upon a most elegant rising ground on the banks of the Potomac, ten miles from Alexandria. We arrived at Mount Vernon by one o'clock—so called by the General's eldest brother, who lived there before him, after the admiral of that name.[3]

When Colonel Fitzgerald introduced me to the General, I was struck with his noble and venerable appearance. It immediately brought to my mind the great part he had acted in the late war. The General is about six foot high, perfectly straight and well made, rather inclined to be lusty. His eyes are full and blue and seem to express an air of gravity. His nose inclines to the aquiline; his mouth small; his teeth are yet good; and his cheeks indicate perfect health. His forehead is a noble one, and he wears his hair turned back, without curls (quite in the officer's style) and tied in a long queue behind. Altogether, he makes a most noble, respectable appearance, and I really think him the first man in the world. After having had the management and care of the whole Continental Army, he has now retired without receiving any pay for his trouble. And though solicited by the King of France and some of the first characters in the world to visit Europe he has denied them all and knows how to prefer solid happiness in his retirement to all the luxuries and flattering speeches of European courts.

The General was born and educated near Fredericksburg on the Rappahannock. He must be a man of great abilities and a strong natural genius, as his master never taught him anything but writing and arithmetic. People come to see him here from all parts of the world; hardly a day passes without. But the General seldom makes his appearance before dinner, employing the morning to write his letters and superintend his farm, and allotting the afternoon to company. But even then he generally retires for two hours, between tea and supper, to his study to write.

He is one of the most regular men in the world. When no particular company is at his house, he goes to bed always at nine, and gets up with the sun. It's astonishing the packets of letters that daily come for him, from all parts of the world, which employ him most of the morning to answer, and his secretary Mr. Shaw[4] (an acquaintance of mine) to copy and arrange. The General has all the accounts of the war yet to settle. Shaw tells me he keeps as regular books as any merchant whatever—and a daily journal of all his transactions. It's amazing the number of letters he wrote during the war. There are thirty large folio volumes of them upstairs, as big as common ledgers, all neatly copied. The General is remarked for writing a most elegant letter. Like the famous Addison, his writing excels his speaking.

But to finish this long digression—when I was first introduced to him, he was neatly dressed in a plain blue coat, white cassimere waistcoat, and black breeches and boots, as he came from his farm. After having sit with us some time, he retired and sent in his lady, a most agreeable woman about fifty, and Major Washington, his nephew, married about three weeks ago to a Miss Besset.[5] She is Mrs. Washington's niece, and a most charming young woman; she is about nineteen. After chatting with them for half an hour, the General came in again, with his hair neatly powdered, a clean shirt on, a new plain, drab coat, white waistcoat, and white silk stockings.

At three dinner was on table, and we were shown by the General into another room, where everything was set off with a peculiar taste and at the same time very neat and plain. The General sent the bottle about pretty freely after dinner, and gave success to the navigation of the Potomac for his toast, which he has very much [at] heart, and when finished will, I suppose, be the first river in the world. He never undertakes anything without having first well considered of it and consulted different people. But when once he has begun anything, no obstacle or

Martha Washington, a portrait by an unknown artist, ca. 1800–25.
(Courtesy of the National Portrait Gallery, Smithsonian Institution)

difficulty can come in his way but what he is determined to surmount. The General's character seems to be a prudent but a very persevering one. He is quite pleased at the idea of the Baltimore merchants laughing at him and saying it was a ridiculous plan and would never succeed. They begin now, says the General, to look a little serious about the matter, as they know it must hurt their commerce amazingly.

The Colonel and I had our horses ready after dinner to return to Alexandria, and, notwithstanding all we could do, the General absolutely insisted upon our staying, on account of the bad afternoon. We therefore complied—although it was fully my intention to have set off either to Fredericksburg in my way to Mr. McCall's in the stage, if the morning was fine, and if not most certainly back again to Baltimore—as I could not refuse the pressing and kind invitation of so great a general. Though our greatest enemy, I admire him as superior even to the Roman heroes themselves.

After tea the General Washington retired to his study and left us with the President, his lady, and the rest of the company. If he had not been anxious to hear the news of Congress from Mr. Lee, most probably he would not have returned to supper but gone to bed at his usual hour, nine o'clock—for he seldom makes any ceremony. We had a very elegant supper about that time.

The General with a few glasses of champagne got quite merry, and being with his intimate friends laughed and talked a good deal. Before strangers, he is generally very reserved and seldom says a word. I was fortunate in being in his company with his particular acquaintances. I'm told during the war he was never seen to smile. The care indeed of such an army was almost enough to make anybody thoughtful and grave. No man but the General could have kept the army together without victuals or clothes. They placed a confidence in him that they would have had in no other person. His being a man of great fortune and having no children showed them it was quite a disinterested part that [he] was acting with regard to money-making, and that he only had the good of his country at heart. The soldiers, though starving at times, in a manner adored him.

We had a great deal of conversation about the slippery ground, as the

General said, that Franklyn was on;[6] and also about Congress, the Potomac, improving their roads, etc.

At twelve I had the honor of being lighted up to my bedroom by the General himself. . . .

[The following day] I rose early and took a walk about the General's grounds, which are really beautifully laid out. He has about 4,000 acres,[7] well cultivated, and superintends the whole himself. Indeed, his greatest pride now is to be thought the first farmer in America. He is quite a Cincinnatus, and often works with his men himself: strips off his coat and labors like a common man.

The General has a great turn for mechanics. It's astonishing with what niceness he directs everything in the building way, condescending even to measure the things himself, that all may be perfectly uniform. The style of his house is very elegant, something like the Prince de Conde's at Chantilli near Paris, only not quite so large. But it's a pity he did not build a new one at once, as it has cost him nearly as much repairing his old one. His improvements, I'm told, are very great within this last year. He is making a most delightful bowling green before the house, and cutting a new road through the woods to Alexandria.

It would be endless to attempt describing his house and grounds. I must content myself with having seen them. The situation is a heavenly one, upon one of the finest rivers in the world. I suppose I saw thousands of wild ducks upon it, all within gunshot. There are also plenty of blackbirds and wild geese and turkeys. After breakfast I went with Shaw to see his famous racehorse, "Magnolia," a most beautiful creature. A whole length of him [Washington] was taken a little while ago, mounted on "Magnolia," by a famous man from Europe, in copper, and his bust in marble—one by order of Congress, to be kept wherever they sit, and the other by the state of Virginia, to stand in the House of Assembly. They will cost about six thousand sterling, Shaw says. He also showed me an

This rare eighteenth-century view of the east front of the mansion and grounds, attributed to Edward Savage, 1792, shows the mansion on the bluff overlooking the Potomac
River. The two-story building to the right of the large tree is a slave dwelling, known as
the house for families, which was torn down soon after this painting was completed.
The adjacent one-story structure is also a slave quarter, while the back of the two-story
greenhouse appears at the far right. The red brick wall in the center of the painting is a
ha-ha, the top and bottom of which are level with the lawn and a lower field, respectively; the structure kept livestock and wild animals away from the house. At the left,
between the Potomac and the lawn of the mansion, is Washington's deer park.
(Courtesy of the Mount Vernon Ladies' Association)

elegant state carriage, with beautiful emblematical figures on it, made
him a present of by the state of Pennsylvania.

I afterwards went into his stables, where among an amazing number
of horses I saw old "Nelson," now twenty-two years of age, that carried
the General almost always during the war. "Blueskin," another fine old
horse next to him, now and then had that honor. Shaw also showed me
his old servant, that was reported to have been taken with a number of
the General's papers about him. They have heard the roaring of many a
cannon in their time. "Blueskin" was not the favorite, on account of his

This painting, also attributed to Edward Savage, 1792, shows the west front
of the mansion and lawn at the height of their eighteenth-century development.
The plain, functional plantation house that Washington inherited has been trans-
formed into a gracious country estate, with a much enlarged dwelling connected
by arcades to outbuildings. Samuel Vaughan drew a complete schema of the
mansion and its immediate surrounds in 1787 (see the map on p. 49).
(Courtesy of the Mount Vernon Ladies' Association)

not standing fire so well as venerable old "Nelson." The General makes
no manner of use of them now; he keeps them in a nice stable, where
they feed away at their ease for their past services. There is a horse of
Major Washington's there that was reckoned the finest figure in the
American army.

It's astonishing what a number of small houses the General has upon
his estate for his different workmen and Negroes to live in. He has everything within himself—carpenters, bricklayers, brewers, blacksmiths,
bakers, etc., etc.—and even has a well-assorted store for the use of his

family and servants. When the General takes his coach out he always drives six horses; to his chariot he only puts four. The General has some fine deer, which he is going to inclose a park for;[8] also some remarkable large foxhounds, made him a present of from England, as he is fond of hunting and there are great plenty of foxes in this country.

I forgot to mention Mrs. Washington's sweet little grandchildren,[9] who, [I] imagine, will come in for a share of the General's fortune, with the Major. I fancy he is worth £100,000 sterling, and lives at the rate of three or four thousand a year—always keeping a genteel table for strangers that almost daily visit him, as a thing of course. There is a fine family picture, in the drawing room, of the Marquis de la Fayette, his lady, and three children; another, of the General with his marching orders when he was Colonel Washington in the British army against the French in the last war;[10] and two of Mrs. Washington's children (her son was reckoned one of the handsomest men living)—also a picture of Mrs. Washington when a young woman. The General has some hundreds of Negroes on his plantations. He chiefly grows Indian corn, wheat, and tobacco.

It's astonishing with what raptures Mrs. Washington spoke about the discipline of the army—the excellent order they were in, superior to any troops, she said, upon the face of the earth, towards the close of the war. Even the English acknowledge it, she said. What pleasure she took in the sound of the fifes and drums, preferring it to any music that was ever heard! And then to see them reviewed a week or two before they were disbanded, when they were all well clothed, was, she said, a most heavenly sight. Almost every soldier shed tears at parting with the General, when the army was disbanded. Mrs. Washington said it was a most melancholy sight.

The situation of Mount Vernon is by nature one of the sweetest in the world, and what makes it still more pleasing is the amazing number of sloops that are constantly sailing up and down the river. Indeed, all the

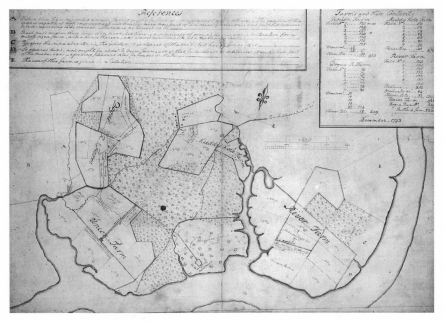

George Washington's survey map, 1793, delineates the five farms
into which he divided Mount Vernon. (Reproduced by permission
of the Henry E. Huntington Library, San Marino, Calif.)

ships that come to Alexandria or George Town must sail by the Generals
house.

At eleven we took leave of him. I shook him heartily by the hand and
wished him all happiness.

1. Colonel John Fitzgerald of Alexandria.

2. Richard Henry Lee of Virginia.

3. Lawrence Washington, GW's half brother, named the estate after the British
admiral Edward Vernon, with whom he had served in the Caribbean in the 1740s.

4. William Shaw became GW's secretary in the summer of 1785.

5. George Augustine Washington married Frances ("Fanny") Bassett at Mount
Vernon in October 1785. He helped GW manage the estate.

6. Benjamin Franklin was then embroiled in the politics of Pennsylvania, a notoriously contentious state during the Revolutionary era.

7. By the 1780s the estate encompassed approximately eight thousand acres. People frequently over- or underestimated its size.

8. GW's deer park was located below the mansion and along the Potomac River. It can be seen in the lower left corner of the 1792 painting of the east front of the mansion and grounds (see the illustration on p. 32). The low-lying walls, called ha-has, kept animals at a distance from the house.

9. Eleanor Parke Custis and George Washington Parke Custis, who lived at Mount Vernon. Their father, John Parke Custis (Martha Washington's son from her first marriage), died of camp fever contracted during the Yorktown campaign in 1781.

10. The Seven Years' War (1756–63), in which GW began his military career as an officer in the Virginia Regiment.

1786

Laboring Hands
George Washington

Whereas visitors typically described the appearance of Mount Vernon and the hospitality received at the estate, only occasionally did they also comment on the African American slaves who waited on Washington family members and their guests, maintained the buildings and grounds, and worked the fields. One of the largest slave owners in Virginia, Washington counted 216 men, women, and children at Mount Vernon on 18 February 1786.

That rare census is reproduced here. Slaves whom he designated with an asterisk belonged to the estate of Martha Washington's first husband, Daniel Parke Custis; those whom Washington owned outright were acquired through inheritance, purchase, and births to his female slaves. The census locates each person on the Home House (mansion) grounds or one of four outlying plantations and a gristmill, which together com-

prised the eight-thousand-acre estate. Slave overseers managed the crews on three farms, and female agricultural workers outnumbered males. The census provides only partial information about family connections. That is, young children's mothers are identified but not their fathers or older siblings.

That same winter of 1785–86, Washington began keeping a weekly account of work accomplished on each farm unit, as well as the status of his livestock. Hired managers subsequently continued the practice, even during his presidency. (With some exaggeration Congressman William Maclay in 1790 likened the plantation to a military operation: "not a days Work, but is noted What, by Whom, and Where done. not a Cow calves or Ewe drops her lamb, but is registered. deaths &ca. Whether accidental or by the hands of the Butcher, all minuted. Thus the etiquette and arrangement of an army is preserved on his farm.") Following the slave census are two farm reports, also written in February 1786. They bring into graphic relief the amount of manual labor required of both female and male slaves.

The list of slaves is in *The Diaries of George Washington*, edited by Donald Jackson and Dorothy Twohig, 6 vols. (Charlottesville, Va., 1976–79), 4:277–83. The farm reports are in *The Papers of George Washington: Confederation Series*, edited by W. W. Abbot et al., 6 vols. (Charlottesville, Va., 1992–97), 3:396–98, and are reprinted with permission of the University of Virginia Press. The Maclay quotation is in *The Diary of William Maclay and Other Notes on Senate Debates*, edited by Kenneth R. Bowling and Helen E. Veit (Baltimore, Md., 1988), 258.

List of Slaves: February 1786

Took a list to day of all my Negroes which are as follows at Mount Vernon and the plantations around it—viz.—

Home House.

Will	Val de Chambre	1
Frank *Austin	} Waiters in the House	2
Herculus Nathan	} Cooks	2
Giles *Joe Paris—boy	} Drivers, & Stablers	3
*Doll *Jenny	} almost past Service	2
*Betty *Lame Alice *Charlotte	} Sempstresses	3
*Sall *Caroline	} House Maids	2
Sall Brass *Dolly	} Washers	2
*Alce Myrtilla *Kitty Winny	} Spinners	4
*Schomberg	old & almost blind past labour	1
Frank Cook Jack	Stock keeper old Jobber	2
Gunner Boatswain Sam Anthony *Tom Davis *Will *Joe	} Labourers	7
Jack	Waggoner	1
*Simms	Carter	1
Bristol	Gardener	1
Isaac James Sambo *Tom Nokes	} Carpenters	4

During Benjamin Henry Latrobe's visit to the estate in the summer of 1796, he drew this "Sketch of a Group for a Drawing." A slave waits on Eleanor Parke Custis (standing), who was the granddaughter of Martha Washington and was raised at Mount Vernon, and (seated) two unidentified figures. (Courtesy of the Maryland Historical Society, Baltimore)

Natt				
George	} Smiths			2
*Peter—lame	Knitter			1
			grown	41

Children

*Oney	Betty's	House	12 yrs. old	
*Delphy	Ditto		6 do.	2
*Anna	little Alice's		13 do.	
*Christopher	Do.		11 do.	
*Judy	Do.		7 do.	
*Vina	Do.		5 do.	4
*Sinah	Kitty's		14 do.	
*Mima	Ditto		12 do.	
*Ally	Ditto		10 do.	

*Lucy	Ditto	8 do.	
*Grace	Ditto	6 do.	
*Letty	Ditto	4 do.	
*Nancy	Ditto	2 do.	7
*Richmond	Lame Alce	9 do.	
*Evey	Do.	2 do.	
*Delia	Do.	3 mo.	3
Lilly	Myrtilla's	11 yrs. old	
Ben	Ditto	8 do.	
Harry	Do.	3 do.	
Boatswain	Do.	6 do.	
Lally	Do.	3 mo.	5
*Cyrus	Sall's	11 do.	1
*Timothy	Charlottes	1 do.	1
*Wilson	Caroline	1 do.	1
*Moll	⎱ Mr. Custis's Estate		2
*Peter	⎰	In all	67

Mill

Ben	Miller	1
Jack	⎫	
Tom	⎬ Cowpers	3
Davy	⎭	
	In all	4

River Plantn.

*Davy	Overseer	1
*Breechy	⎫	
Nat		
Ned		
Essex		
Bath		
*Johny	⎬ Labourg. Men	10
Adam	dead	
*Will		
Robin		
*Ben	⎭	
*Molly	Overseers Wife	1

Ruth
*Dolly
Peg
Daphne
Murria
*Agnus
Suck
Sucky
Judy—M   } labourg. Women   17
Judy—F
*Hannah
*Cornelia
*Lidia
*Esther
Cloe
*Fanny
*Alice

grown   29

Children

Will	Mill Judy's	——13 yrs. old	1
*Joe	Hannahs	——12 Do.	1
Ben	Peg's	10 Do.	
Penny	Ditto	—— 8 Do.	2
Joe	Daphne's	8 do.	
Moses	Ditto	6 do.	
Lucy	Ditto	4 do.	
Daphne	Ditto	—— 1 do.	4
*Ned	Lidia's	7 do.	
*Peter	Ditto	5 do.	
*Phoebe	Ditto	—— 3 do.	3
Cynthia	Suckey's	6 do.	
Daniel	Ditto	—— 4 do.	2
*James	Ferry Doll's	8 do.	1
*Bett	Neck Dolls	7 do.	
*Natt	Ditto	4 do.	
*Dolly	Ditto	3 do.	
*Jack	Ditto	—— 1 do.	4
Rose	Suck-Bass	12 do.	1

41

*Milly	House Sall's	7 do.	1
*Billy	Do. Charlottes	4 do.	1
*Hukey	Agnus's	1 do.	1
*Ambrose	Cornelia's	1 month	1
		In all	52

Dogue Run — Plantn.

*Morris	Overseer	1
Robin Adam Jack Jack — long Dick Ben *Matt *Morris	Labourg. Men	8
*Brunswick	Ruptured	1
Hannah	Overrs. wife	1
*Lucy Moll Jenny Silla Charity *Betty *Peg *Sall *Grace *Sue	Labourg. Women old	10
	grown	21

Children

Sarah	Charity's	6 yrs. old	
Billy	Ditto	5 do.	
Hannah	Ditto	3 do.	
Elly	Ditto	6 mo.	4
*Jesse	Salls	6 yrs. old	

*Kitty	Do.	4 do.	
*Lawrence	Do.	1 do.	3
*Jenny	Lucy's	9 do.	
*Daniel	Do.	3 do.	
*Ned	Do.	6 Mo.	3
Aggy	Jones (dead)	9 yrs. old	
Simon	Do.	4 do.	
Bett	Do.	3 do.	3
Sophia	Sylla's	3 do.	
Sabra	Ditto	6 Mo.	2
*Andrew	Bettys'	1 yr. old	1
*Crager	Pegs	6 Mo.	1
		In all	38

Ferry—Plantn.

*Sam Kit ⎫		
London ⎪		
*Caesar ⎬	labourg. Men	5
*Cupid ⎪		
*Paul ⎭		
*Betty ⎫		
*Doll ⎬	labourg. Women	3
*Lucy ⎭		
*Lucy ⎫		
Flora ⎪		
*Fanny ⎪		
*Rachel ⎬	Labouring Women	7
*Jenny ⎪		
Edy ⎪		
*Daphne ⎭		
	grown	15

Children

*Godfrey	Betty's	12 yrs. old	
*Beck	Ditto	11 do.	
*Hanson	Ditto	7 do.	
*Lucretia	Ditto	6 do.	
*John	Ditto	3 do.	
*Bill langston	Ditto	6 Mo.	6

*Patt	Doll's	11 yrs. old	
*Milly	Ditto	4 do.	
*Daniel	Ditto	3 do.	
*Silvia	Ditto	1 do.	4
*Edmund	Lucy	6 do.	
*Mike	Ditto	3 do.	
*Phill	Ditto	8 Mo.	3
Joy	Flora	8 yrs. old	
Jacob	Ditto	5 do.	2
		In all	30

Muddy hole Plann.

*Will		
*Will		
Charles	Labourg. Men	5
Gabriel		
*Jupiter		
Kate		
Nanny		
Sarah		
Alice		
Peg	labourg. Women	9
Sackey		
Darcus		
Amy		
Nancy		
	grown	14

Children

Molly	Kates	14 yrs. old	
Virgin	Ditto	11 do.	
Will	Ditto	8 do.	
Kate	Ditto	4 do.	4
Moses	Darcuss	8 do.	
Townshend	Do.	6 Mo.	2
Letty	Peg's	7 yrs. old	
Forrister	Ditto	2 do.	2
Uriah	Sackey's	10 do.	1

Kate	Alice's	4	do.		1
Isbel	Sarah's	3	do.		1
	Muddy hole	.	.	. In all	25
	Home House				67
	River Plantation				52
	Dogue Run Plantn.				38
	Ferry Plantation				30
N.B. Those marked	Mill				4
with asterisks are				Total	216
Dower Negros.					

Farm Reports: February 1786

River Plantation Feb. 4th

Monday, Women Threshin—Men (except Essex who was making Baskets for home house) Morticing posts. Tuesday, Women making fence round Timberlanding field; Men cutting and Mauling—Wednesday—Ditto—D[itt]o—Thursday the same—Friday same. Saturday Women Toating leaves into the Farm pen—Then, assisting in removing Houses[1] at Mt Vernon. & then making a pen to feed Jocky hogs the year round—One old Cow dead—& one Calf came. 10 lambs—Carts getting rails to fence—2 days Plowing with 4 plows.

Dogue Run. 4th Feby

Men Cutting & Mauling as usual. Women making new fence along the Wood to the Corner by the old gate, & from thence to the present Wheat field fence with old rails—lodging[2] all the New ground in order to Hoe, all—also did part of the fence from the New fence towards the Meadow fence by the House. plowed a little yesterday and today within the enclosure of the upper meadow—2 lambs Yeaned this week & one died—25 in all—6 Calves in all—an old Oxe Pompey dead. The old mares mending.

Carpenters—4th Feby

42 White Oak Saplins for sheep fold—125 bars rived for D[itt]o 2 trees cut down & 4 cuts taken of one for Do—11 forks for removing the Garden Houses—12 Stocks 10 feet long 12½ Inches Square—2 of which sawed.

Ferry Plantation 4th Feby

Women Grubbing except Flora, who was sick—2 Men getting rails for the Plantation—2 Lambs and 1 Calf this Week—all the rest of the Stock as usual. Ferry men (when not in the Boat) cutting where the women are Grubbing.

Muddy hole Plantn 4th Feb.

41 Sheep—17 Lambs (one yeaned this Week) 32 Cattle—22 Horses— Women grubbing all the week with the overseer. little Will plowed half a day Monday, tuesday, Wednesday & thursday, & all friday. & part of this day after going from M. Vernon. Charles & Jupiter Mauling, Will cutting Rails &ca when not plowing—Cart drawing Rails round fence yesterday, & part of this day.

. . . .

Dogue Run—18th Feby

Monday hoed up ground with the Women. Men cleaning up the swamps—cleared up the ground where the Hog pen was & continued the cross fence toward the Ho[me] House meadow as far as the logs would go. cleaning & burning up the swamps—Men during the bad weather hueing Posts. One Lamb this week (28 in all)—Black Mare in the lift all the rest of the stock well.

River Plantation 18th Feb.

Monday filling up Gullies with the Women—5 days threshing with D[itt]o—Monday 7 plows running. 4 men cutting & mauling in the

Woods—Tuesday Men morticing Posts; & 4 days cutting & mauling in the woods. 2 Carts hauling Rails 4 days & the Waggon two days—8 Lambs this Week—1 Calf.

Carpenters—18th Feby

66 Mortices dug two Inches wide & 6 Inches deep 80 Tenants made 1 Inch thick—300 laths rived of pine—2 Corner posts got today & sawed for the inclosures for the stud horses—Isaac lame all this week and last.

Ferry Platn 18th Feby

1 Fellow plowing & cutting straw all the Week. 1 D[itt]o Mauling and loading the Waggon with Hay 1 Do employed Carting—Sam & London when not at the ferry employed Cutting—and all the Wom[e]n grubbing this Week—Stock all well, & as usual—1 Lamb this Week.

1. As part of his efforts to beautify his plantation and make it an inspirational model for the citizenry of the entire United States, GW had the gardens enlarged and enhanced. That necessitated moving several garden houses.

2. Beating down the remains of previous crops.

1787

A MODEL FOR THE NATION
Samuel Powel

Samuel Powel and his wife, Elizabeth Willing Powel, of Philadelphia, were friends of the Washingtons and stayed at Mount Vernon in October 1787. Mr. Powel's journal entry for their visit contains a rather full description of the appearance of the estate and, in addition, reflects the men's mutual passion for agriculture. A former mayor of Philadelphia,

Powel had recently been elected the first president of the Philadelphia Society for Promoting Agriculture.

A photocopy of this journal excerpt is among the holdings of the Mount Vernon Ladies' Association and is used with permission. Extensive efforts to locate the original journal were unsuccessful.

At Three O'Clock we left this Place [Alexandria] for Mount Vernon the Seat of his Excellency General Washington distant Nine Miles & rode thro' a hilly Country & good Roads. We arrived there to Tea & were most cordially received by the General & Mrs. Washington. The approach to this Seat is very pleasing. At the Entrance from the Road you have a View of the House at the Distance of near a Mile. The Grounds on each Side of the Road are cleared of the under wood & the Saplings neatly trimmed so as to promise to form a handsome Wood in future. Passing thro' this young Wood the Road lies thro' a bottom till you approach the House. After ascending the Eminence on which the Mansion is placed you enter a very large Court Yard, with a pavilion on each Side & proceed thro' a circular Road covered with rough Gravel till you come to the Offices, from which the Road is paved to the House. Within this road the ground is covered with Grass. The House has an uniform appearance, is about an hundred feet in Front with a Turrett[1] on the Top. The Building is of Wood cut in Squares to resemble Courses of Stone, which is painted & sanded so as to imitate Stone, & may easily be mistaken for it. The whole appearance of the Garden front is handsome, tho' not altogether regular as to the Windows under the Pediment having been built at different Times. It is joined to the Offices by Colonades with Arches painted green.

In the inside you enter a Hall in which the Stair Case is placed. On each Side of this Hall are two Rooms. At the east west End of the House is a magnificent Room Sixteen feet high of perhaps thirty Seven by Twenty Eight Feet, with a Window to the North & South, a venetian

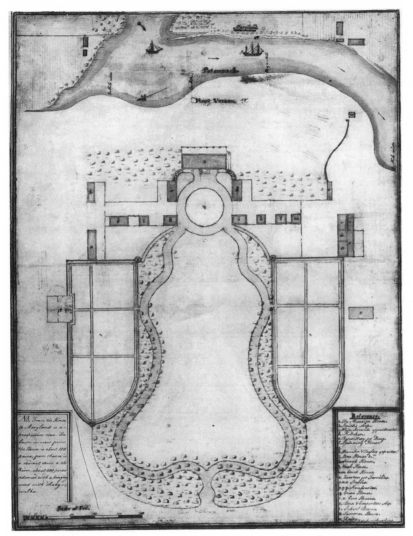

Samuel Vaughan's plan of the mansion and grounds, 1787. This drawing shows
the result of improvements that Washington designed, including an enlarged house, a
circular bowling green, serpentine pathways, and, beside them, bullet-shaped gardens.
(Courtesy of the Mount Vernon Ladies' Association)

The largest and most elegant room in the house is the large dining room, with its Palladian-style windows. Washington supervised the initial work on this room before going off to war in 1775, and he oversaw its completion after his return home in 1783. Here the Washingtons entertained many of their guests. (Photograph, 2003, courtesy of the Mount Vernon Ladies' Association)

This Italian marble mantel, a gift of Samuel Vaughan of Philadelphia,
is the most elaborate architectural feature in the mansion. It stands opposite
the Palladian-style windows in the large dining room. Vaughan also presented
the Washingtons with the porcelain pieces that stand on the mantel.
(Photograph, 1991, courtesy of the Mount Vernon Ladies' Association)

Window to the East.[2] The Chimney piece is of Italian Marble with
Columns of Sienna Marble & very handsome bas relief Tablets of white
marble, relative to rural Affairs. It would have been handsomer without
the Columns. The Room is the whole h[e]ight of the House. The Cieling
is cove[re]d & richly ornamented in a light pleasing Taste.

The West End contains a very handsome Study,[3] private Stair Case &
Apartments over the Study for the General[, which] is retired and

detached from the Family, which considering the perpetual & elegant Hospitality exercised here is absolutely requisite.

The front toward the river is ornamented with a deep Portico supported by eight square Columns & paved with Whitehaven Flags[tone]. This is a delightful place to walk in & admirably adapted to the Climate. It is of the whole height of the House, & necessarily renders the chambers dark. The House is most beautifully seated on the high commanding Bank of the Patowmack, which is here about a mile and an half Broad. On the declivity between the House & the River is a park with Deer. The View down the River is extensive & most charming. Nearly opposite the House the River Piscataway empties itself into the majestic Patowmack & adds greatly to the beauty of the Scene. In a Word this is altogether the most charming Seat I have seen in America. It is kept with great Neatness & the good Order of the Masters Mind appears extended to every Thing around it. Tradesmen of every kind necessary for a farm are to be found here. This estate consists of about Eight Thousand Acres. The Family consists of the General, his Lady, Major George Washington & his Lady a very pleasing fine Woman, & Master & Miss Custis, Mrs. Washington's grand Children.

Sunday 7. Spent this Day very agreeably in Conversation & admiring the Beauties of Mount Vernon. At Dinner Time & while we were at Table Mr. Bushrod Washington & his Wife arrived.[4]

Monday 8. After Breakfast I rode with the General over several of his Farms. Mrs. Washington & Mrs. Powel accompanied us to the Mill, which is a very good one. The long & severe Drought which this Country has experienced has rendered the Appearance of these Farms unfavorable. The General informed me that he had about Three Thousand Acres in Tillage, that he had in some Years raised near Fifteen Thousand Bushells of Indian Corn & I think three Thousand Bushells of wheat but that this Year his Crops would not exceed fifteen hundred Bushells of

Corn & one Thousand Bushells of Wheat, & that the Wheat was so infested by the Weavill that he was obliged to thrash it out, & was trying an Experiment to preserve it by mixing it with quick Lime. To supply the deficiency of his Crops he had sown large Quantities of Buckwheat & forty Acres of field Peas, broadcast. They have both been injured by the Frost. There is no Tobacco planted on this Estate.

Tuesday 9. Rode with the general & the Ladies to view a Seat of Col. Fairfax, Seven Miles distant, beautifully situated on the Patowmack.[5] The House which was of brick is burnt, & the Walls only standing. On our return we visited some of the Farms. The Peas are now cutting & the Grain treading out. The General pays great Attention to husbandry & is, with reason I believe, said to be the best Farmer in the State.

Wednesday 10. Left Mount Vernon, with some regret after our polite, friendly & agreeable Entertainment there. The greatest Decorum reigns at this Place & every Thing is most pleasingly conducted. The General was so obliging as to send us to Colchester, Ten Miles in his own Carriage, where we arrived about Nine & met our own Carriage which we had sent on the Evening before.

1. The cupola.

2. Powel's positioning of the house is incorrect. The "magnificent" room (the Palladian-style dining room) is at the north side of the house.

3. The study is on the south end of the house.

4. GW's nephew Bushrod married Julia Ann Blackburn, of Prince William County, Virginia.

5. The Fairfax estate built by Colonel William Fairfax was named Belvoir. The mansion burned in 1783.

1788

DINNER AND TALK OF THE NEW CONSTITUTION
Olney Winsor

In March 1788, merchant Olney Winsor, then living in Alexandria, and several other townsmen were invited to dine with the Washingtons. At that time, only six states had ratified the Federal Constitution drafted at Philadelphia the previous summer. Winsor was from Rhode Island, where ratification seemed in doubt. Lively after-dinner conversation ensued, as he recounted in this letter to his wife, Hope Winsor, who remained in New England.

This letter, dated 31 March, is located in the Miscellaneous Manuscripts Collection, Rhode Island Historical Society, Providence, and is used with permission.

Saturday morning last Mr Jenckes & myself received a very polite Card from General Washington, requesting our company to dine with him on Sunday, in Company with several other Gentlemen from this Town. Accordingly we set out from the Store yesterday Morning half past 11. oClock and arrived at Mount Vernon about one, where we were received by the General & his family with great freedom and politeness, at the same time without any ceremonious parade. The general converses with great deliberation, & with ease, except in pronouncing some few words, in which he has a hesitancy of speech. He was dressed in a plain drab Coat, red Jacket, buff Breeches & white Hose.

Mrs. Washington is an elegant figure for a person of her Years, perhaps 45. She is rather fleshy, of good complexion, has a large portly double chin, and an open & engageing Countenance, on which a pleasing smile sets during Conversation, in which she bears an agreeable part.

She was dressed in a plain black Satten Gown, with long sleves, figured Lawn apron & Handkf, guaze french night Cap with black bowes—all very neat—but not guady.

From this description you will conclude that your *plain* Husband was pleased with his reception, and felt himself perfectly at ease, in this agreable & improveing Company.

We had an exceeding good Dinner, which was served up in excellent order. After Dinner the new Constitution was introduced as the subject of conversation, & sundry questions asked me by the General, & Colo. Humphreys,[1] from Connecticut, who now resides at the Generals, respecting the part I expected your State [Rhode Island] would take. I wish I could have given them more pleasing answers, but we all hoped for the best. The General expressed himself on the Subject with such real concern for the united happiness of the States, & at the same time with such clearness on those parts of the Constitution which have been objected to, as not being suffic[ie]ntly explicit, that I was as much pleased with him, as a private man, a former of a System for the United States, as I have heretofore been in his military character, in which all agree that he was the Saviour of America. Then, how preposterous a part do those now act, who charge him with being a Conspirator against the liberties of that very Country which he so lately saved from the all grasping hand of a haughty Tyrant.[2] To start the Idea is ungratefull, to divulge it, is black infernal ingratitude!

We left the agreable circle at the Generals about half past 5. oClock & arrived at the Store about Seven.

1. David Humphreys, formerly an aide-de-camp to GW.
2. Winsor was referring to strident Anti-Federalist opponents of the draft Constitution.

1796

"WASHINGTON HAS SOMETHING UNCOMMONLY MAJESTIC AND COMMANDING IN HIS WALK, HIS ADDRESS, HIS FIGURE AND HIS COUNTENANCE"

Benjamin Henry Latrobe

Although the flow of visitors understandably slowed during Washington's presidency, when the national capital was at Philadelphia, he told his farm manager that he did not object "to any sober or orderly person's gratifying their curiosity in viewing the buildings, Gardens &ca. about Mount Vernon."[1] During a brief stay at home in the summer of 1796, the Washingtons welcomed Benjamin Henry Latrobe, the English-born engineer and architect. He not only wrote one of the most informative eighteenth-century accounts of a visit to Mount Vernon but also produced several sketches. The president clearly enjoyed talking with his talented guest, and Latrobe, a keen observer, recorded much of the substance of their wide-ranging conversations. He was impressed with the unpretentiousness of the Washingtons.

This account appears in *The Virginia Journals of Benjamin Henry Latrobe, 1795–1798*, edited by Edward C. Carter II et al., 2 vols. (New Haven, Conn., 1977), 1:161–72, © Yale University Press, and is used with permission.

On Sunday the 16th of July, I set off on horseback for Mount Vernon, having a letter to the President from his Nephew my particular friend Bushrod Washington Esq. I travelled through a bold broken country to Colchester.[2] Colchester lies on the North Side of the river Occoquan over which there is a ferry. The river is filled chiefly by the back Water of the Potowmac. . . . From Colchester to Mount Vernon the road lies through extensive woods. The distance is about ten miles. About 2½ Miles from the President's house is a Mill belonging to him on a Canal brought from the river Dogue.[3] Its neatness is an indication of the attention of the owner to his private concerns. The farm of the President extends from the Mill to his house. Good fences, clear grounds and extensive cultivation strike the eye as something uncommon in this part of the World but the road is bad enough. The house becomes visible between two Groves of trees at about a miles distance. It has no very striking appearance, though superior to every other house I have seen here. The approach is not very well managed but leads you into the area between the Stables. . . . It is a wooden building, painted to represent champhered [beveled] rustic and sanded. The center is an old house to which a good dining room has been added at the North end, and a study &c. &c., at the South. The House is connected with the Kitchen offices by arcades. The whole of this part of the building is in a very indifferent taste. Along the other front is a portico supported by 8 square pillars, of good proportions and effect. There is a handsome statuary marble chimney piece in the dining room (of the taste of Sir Wm. Chambers), with insulated columns on each side. This is the only piece of expensive decoration I have seen about the house, and is indeed *remarkable* in that respect.[4] Every thing else is extremely good and neat, but by no means above what would be expected in a plain English Country Gentleman's house of £500 or £600 a Year. It is however a little above what I have hitherto seen in Virginia. The ground on the West front of the house is laid out in a level lawn bounded on each side with a wide but extremely formal serpentine walk, shaded by weeping Willows, a tree which in this country grows very well upon high dry land. On one side of this lawn is a plain Kitchen garden, on the other a neat flower garden laid out in squares, and boxed with great precission. Along the North Wall of this Garden is a plain Greenhouse. The Plants were arranged in front, and contained nothing very rare, nor were they numerous. For the first time again since I left

Germany, I saw here a parterre, chipped and trimmed with infinite care into the form of a richly flourished Fleur de Lis. . . .

Towards the East Nature has lavished magnificence, nor has Art interfered but to exhibit her to advantage. Before the portico a lawn extends on each hand from the front of the house and of a Grove of Locust trees on each side, to the edge of the bank. Down the steep slope trees and shrubs are thickly planted. They are kept so low as not to interrupt the view but merely to furnish an agreeable border to the extensive prospect beyond. The mighty *Potowmac* runs close under this bank the elevation of which must be perhaps 250 feet. The river is here about 1½ miles across and runs parrallel with the front of the house for about 3 miles to the left and 4 to the right. To the left it takes a sudden turn round a point, and disappears, proceeding to Alexandria and the Foederal City, but the sheet of Water is continued in the Piskattaway[5] which appears at first sight to be the Potowmac, being of the same width. The Piscattaway is in sight to the distance of eight or nine miles and then vanishes at the back of a bold woody headland. This river continues about 15 Miles up the Country a bold Stream, being filled by the back Water of the Potowmac. It is however shallow and at present no object of commercial advantage. An extent of 1500 acres perfectly clear of wood, which borders the river on the left bank on the Virginia side boldly contrasts the remainder of the Woody landscape. It is a farm belonging to the President.[6] The general surface is level, but elevated above all inundations. Beyond this Sheet of verdure the country rises into bold woody hills, sometimes enriched by open plantations, which mount gently above one another till they vanish into the purple distance of the highest ridge 20 miles distant. The Maryland shore has the same character. Opposite to the house, where its detail becomes more distinct it is variegated by lawns and copses.

After running about 4 Miles to the right, the river turns suddenly to the Eastward but is seen over a range of lowland for a considerable dis-

"View of Mount Vernon Looking to the North," by Benjamin Henry Latrobe, 1796.
(Courtesy of the Maryland Historical Society, Baltimore)

tance. A woody peninsula running to a point backs the silver line of the water, and the blue hills of Maryland just appear above the edge of the trees, beyond the next bend. . . .

Having alighted, I sent in my letter of introduction, and walked into the portico next to the river. In about 10 Minutes, the President came to me. He was dressed in a plain blue coat, his hair dressed and powdered. There was a reserve but no hauteur in his manner. He shook me by the hand said he was glad to see a friend of his Nephew, drew a chair and desired me to sit down. Having enquired after the family I had left, the conversation turned upon Bath[7] to which they were going. He said he had known the place when there was scarce a house upon it fit to sleep in. That the accommodations were he believed very good at present. He thought the best thing a family regularly visiting Bath could do, would be to build a house for their separate accomodation, the expence of which might be 200 Pounds. He has himself a house there, which he supposes must be going to ruin. Independent of his public situation the encreased dissipation and frequency of visitors would be an objection to his visiting it again, unless the health of himself or family should render it necessary. At first *that* was the motive, he said, that induced people to encounter the badness of the roads and the inconvenience of the lodgings, but at present few, he believed, in comparison of the whole number, had health in view. Even those whose object it was, were interrupted in their quiet by the dissipation of the rest. This, he observed, must naturally be the case in every large collection of men, whose minds were not occupied by any pressing business or personal interest. In these and many more observations of the same kind, there was no moroseness, nor any thing that appeared as if the rapidly encreasing immorality of the citizens particularly impressed him at the time he made them. They seemed the well expressed remarks of a man who has seen and knows the world.

The conversation then turned upon the rivers of Virginia; he gave me a very minute account of all their directions, their natural advantages, and what he conceived might be done for their improvement by Art. He then enquired whether I had seen the Dismal Swamp and seemed particularly desirous of being informed upon the subject of the Canal going forward there.[8] He gave me a detailed account of the old dismal Swamp [Land] Company and of their operations, of the injury they had received by the effects of the war, and the still greater, which their inattention to their own concerns had done them. After many attempts on his part to procure a meeting of Directors (the number of which the law provided should be *Six* in order to do business), all of which proved fruitless, he gave up all further hopes of any thing effectual being done for their interests, and sold out his shares in the Proprietary at a price very inadequate to their real value. Since then his attention had been so much drawn to public affairs, as scarcely to have made any enquiry into the proceedings either of the Swamp or of the Canal Company. I was much flattered by his attention to my observations, and his taking the pains either to object to my deductions where he thought them illfounded, or to confirm them by very strong remarks of his own, made while he was in the habit of visiting the Swamp.

This conversation lasted above an hour, and as he had at first told me that he was endeavoring to finish some letters to go by the Post upon a variety of business *"which notwithstanding his distance from the Seat of Government still pressed upon him in his retirement:"* I got up to take my leave but he desired me in a manner very like *Dr. [Samuel] Johnson's* to *"keep my chair,"* and then continued to talk to me about the great works going forward in England, and my own objects in this country. I found him well acquainted with my mothers family in Pensylvania. After much conversation upon the Coal-mines on James river I told him of the Silver mine at Rocketts.[9] He laughed most heartily upon the very mention of the thing. I explained to him the nature of the expectations formed of its productiveness and satisfied him of the probability that ore did exist there in considerable Quantity. He made several very minute enquiries concerning it and then said, that; *"it would give him real uneasiness should any silver or gold mine be discovered that would tempt considerable capitals into the prosecution of that object, and that he heartily wished for his country that it might contain no mines 'but such as the plough could reach,' excepting only coal and iron."*

After conversing with me more than two hours he got up and said that *"we should meet again at dinner."* I then strolled about the lawn and took the views. Upon my return to the house, I found Mrs. Washington and her granddaughter Miss Custis in the hall. I introduced myself to Mrs. Washington as a friend of her Nephew, and she immediately entered into conversation upon the prospect from the Lawn and presently gave me an account of her family in a good humoured free manner that was extremely pleasant and flattering. She retains strong remains of considerable beauty, seems to enjoy very good health and to have as good humour. She has no affectation of superiority in the slightest degree, but acts compleatly in the character of the Mistress of the house of a respectable and opulent country gentleman. Her granddaughter Miss Eleanor Custis (the only one of four who is unmarried) has more perfection of form of expression, of color, of softness, and of firmness of mind than I have ever seen before, or conceived consistent with mortality. She is every thing that the chissel of Phidias aimed at, but could not reach; and the soul beaming through her countenance, and glowing in her smile, is as superior to her face, as mind is to matter.

Young la Fayette[10] with his tutor came down sometime before dinner. He is a young man about 17 of a mild pleasant countenance, favorably impressing at first sight. His figure is rather awkward. His manners are easy and he has very little of the usual french air about him. He talked much, especially with Miss Custis and seemed to possess wit, and fluency. He spoke English tolerably well, much better indeed than his tutor who has had the same time and opportunities of improvement.

Dinner was served up about ½ after three. It had been postponed about ½ an hour in hopes of Mr. Lear's[11] arrival from Alexandria. The President came into the portico about ½ an hour before 3 and talked freely upon common topics with the family. At dinner he placed me at the left hand of Mrs. Washington; Miss Custis sat at her right and himself next to her about the middle of the table. There was very little conversation at dinner. A few jokes passed between the President and young la Fayette, whom he treats more as his Child than as a Guest. I felt a little embarrassed at the silent reserved air that prevailed. As I drink no wine and the President drank only 3 glasses the party soon returned to the Portico. Mr. Lear, Mr. Dandridge and Mr. Lear's 3 boys soon after arrived and helped out the conversation. The President retired in about ¾ of an hour.

As much as I wished to stay, I thought it a point of delicacy to take up as little of the time of the president as possible, and I therefore requested Mrs. Washington's permission to order my horses. She expressed a slight wish that I would stay, but I did not think it sufficiently strong *in etiquette* to detain me, and the horses came to the door. I waited a few minutes till the President returned. He asked me whether I had any very pressing business to prevent my lengthening my visit. I told him I had not, but that, as I considered it as an intrusion upon his more important engagements, I thought I could reach Colchester that evening by daylight. "Sir," said he, "you see I take my own way. If you can be content to take yours at my house, I shall be glad to see you here longer."

Coffee was brought, about 6 o'clock. When it was removed the president addressing himself to me enquired after the state of the Crops about Richmond. I told him all I had heard. A long conversation upon farming ensued, during which it grew dark, and he then proposed going into the hall. He made me sit down by him and continued the conversation for above an hour. During that time he gave me a very minute account of the Hessian fly[12] and its progress from long Island where it first appeared through New York, Rhode Island, Connecticut, Delaware, part of Pensylvania and Maryland. It has not yet appeared in Virginia, but is daily dreaded. The cultivation of Indian corn next came up. He dwelt upon all the advantages attending this most usefull crop, and then said that the manner in which the land was exhausted by it, the constant attendance it required during the whole year, and the superior value of the produce of land in other crops would induce him to leave off entirely the cultivation of it, provided he could depend upon any market for a

Supply elsewhere. As food for the Negroes it was his opinion that it was infinitely preferable to Wheat bread in point of Nourishment. He had made the experiment upon his own Lands and had found that though the Negroes, while the Novelty lasted, seemed to prefer Wheat bread as being the food of their Masters, they soon grew tired of it. He conceived that should the negroes be fed upon Wheat or Rye bread, they would, in order to be fit for the same labor, be obliged to have a considerable addition to their allowance of Meat. But notwithstanding all this he thought the balance of advantage to be against the Indian corn.

He then entered into the different merits of a variety of ploughs which he had tried and gave the preference to the heavy Rotheram plough from a full experience of its merits. The Berkshire iron plough he held next in estimation. He had found it impossible to get the iron work of his Rotheram plough replaced in a proper manner otherwise he should never have discontinued its use. I promised to send him one of Mr. Richardson's ploughs of Tuckahoe, which he accepted with pleasure.

Mrs. Washington and Miss Custis had retired early and the President left the company about 8 o'clock. We soon after retired to bed. There was no hint of Supper.

I rose with the Sun, and walked in the grounds near the house. I also took the view. The president came to the company in the sitting room about ½ hour past 7 where all the latest Newspapers were laid out. He talked with Mr. Lear about the progress of the Works at the great falls and in the City of Washington. Breakfast was served up in the usual Virginian style. Tea, Coffee, and cold and broiled Meat. It was very soon over, and for an hour afterwards he stood upon the steps of the West door talking to the Company who were collected round him. The subject was chiefly the establishment of the University at the Foederal City. He mentioned the offer he had made of giving to it all the interests he had in the City on condition that it should go on in a given time, and complained that though magnificent Offers had been made by many Speculators for the same purpose there seemed to be no inclination to carry them into reality. He spoke as if he felt a little hurt upon the Subject. About 10 o'clock he made a motion to retire and I requested a servant to bring my horses to the door. He then returned and as soon as my Servant came up with them he went to him, and asked him if he had breakfasted. He then shook me by the hand desired me to call if I came again into the Neighbourhood, and wished me a good morning.

When my youngest Brother was about six years old he went with the family to see the king of England go through St. James's park in State to the House of Lords. Upon being told that he rode in such and such a carriage, he would scarcely believe that the person he saw could be the king; and being assured that he really was so, he cried out: *"Good lord, papa, how like a man he looks."* The Sentiment *expressed* by the boy, is, I believe, *felt* by every man who sees for the first time a man raised by merit or reputation above the common level of his fellow creatures. It was impressed upon me, upon seeing one of the greatest men that Nature ever produced, but in a less degree than even when I saw that least-like-a-man-looking-king Frederic the Second of Prussia. Washington has something uncommonly majestic and commanding in his walk, his address, his figure and his countenance. His face is characterized however more by intense and powerful thought, than by quick and fiery conception. There is a mildness about its expression; and an air of reserve in his manner lowers its tone still more. He is 64, but appears some years younger, and has sufficient apparent vigor to last many years yet. He was frequently entirely silent for many minutes during which time an awkwardness seemed to prevail in every one present. His answers were often short and sometimes approached to moroseness. He did not at any time speak with very remarkable fluency:—perhaps the extreme correctness of his language which almost seemed studied prevented that effect. He seemed to enjoy a humourous observation, and made several himself. He laughed heartily several times and in a very good humoured manner. On the morning of my departure he treated me as if I had lived for years in his house; with ease and attention, but in general I thought there was a slight air of moroseness about him, as if something had vexed him.

For Washington, had Horace lived at the present age he would have written his celebrated ode: it is impossible to have ever read it and not to recollect in the presence of this great Man the *Virum justum, proposi-tique, tenacem, &c. &c.*[13]

1. GW to William Pearce, 23 Nov. 1794, in *The Writings of George Washington from the Original Manuscript Sources, 1745–1799,* edited by John C. Fitzpatrick, 39 vols. (Washington, D.C., 1931–44), 34:42.

2. Colchester lies south of Mount Vernon, in Fairfax County.

3. Dogue Run Creek.

4. Well into the nineteenth century visitors frequently commented on the elaborately carved marble mantlepiece, which was installed in the large dining room. GW thought the piece, a gift from Samuel Vaughan, excessive for "my republican stile of living." GW to Vaughan, 5 Feb. 1785, in *The Papers of George Washington: Confederation Series,* edited by W. W. Abbot et al., 6 vols. (Charlottesville, Va., 1992–97), 2:326.

5. Piscataway Creek, in Maryland, empties into the Potomac northeast of Mount Vernon.

6. River Farm.

7. Noted for its medicinal springs, Bath was in Berkeley County, Virginia, in an area that GW surveyed as a young man.

8. During the late colonial period entrepreneurs, including GW, dreamed of draining and opening for development thousands of acres of the Dismal Swamp, which straddles the Virginia–North Carolina border.

9. Rackett's Landing near Richmond, Virginia.

10. George Washington Lafayette, the son of General Lafayette, was sent to the United States during the French Revolution and lived with the Washingtons. His parents, however, suffered imprisonment in their homeland.

11. Tobias Lear worked as GW's private secretary.

12. A highly destructive insect, pejoratively named after the German mercenaries whom Great Britain used in the War for Independence.

13. Note from Carter edition: "The man [who is] just and firm in purpose."

1797
"THEY HOPED THEY WOULD NO LONGER
BE SLAVES IN TEN YEARS"
Louis-Philippe

The account of Louis-Philippe is unique because it concentrates entirely on slavery and the lives of Mount Vernon's African Americans. In fact, although the young French nobleman did not devote any space in his travel diary to describing the Washington family, he wrote of conversations with slaves. Louis-Philippe and his party had come to the United States to escape the ravages of the French Revolution. In 1830 he would become king of France under the restored monarchy.

This excerpt is found in *Diary of My Travels in America: Louis-Philippe, King of France, 1830–1848*, translated by Stephen Becker (New York, 1977), 31–32, 35, © 1977 by, and used by permission of, Dell Publishing, a division of Random House, Inc.

The 5th April we had planned to leave in the morning and reach General Washington's home at Mount Vernon in time for dinner, but because some laundry we had sent out was not yet ready, we were compelled to dine in Georgetown, and we were not able to set out until half past four. We crossed on the ferry at Georgetown and arrived at Mount Vernon at half past six, when the general welcomed us with great courtesy. His house is splendidly situated beside the Potowmack, fifteen miles below the city named after him. Though the house is of wood, it looks well, and before it lies what might be a playground carpeted in green. The general owns ten thousand acres of land around Mount Vernon. Hardly half of it is under cultivation. There are about 400 blacks scattered among the different farms.[1] These unfortunates reproduce freely and their number is increasing. I have been thinking that to accomplish their emancipation gradually and without upheaval it might be possible to grant them first a status in mortmain[2] by depriving their owners of the right to sell them. Virginia law imposes the same punishment on a master who kills a slave as on any other murderer, but the law is very rarely applied; as slaves are denied by statute the right to bear witness, the charge is never proved. General Washington has forbidden the use of the whip on his blacks, but unfortunately his example has been little emulated. Here[3] Negroes are not considered human beings. When they meet a white man, they greet him from a distance and with a low bow, and they often seem amazed that we return their greeting, for no one here does so. . . . The general's blacks told Beaudoin[4] that they had clubs in Alexandria and Georgetown, that Quakers came to visit, and that they hoped they would no longer be slaves in ten years—not that they wanted to follow the example of the blacks in Santo-Domingo, they would do no harm to any man, etc.[5] . . . The general's cook ran away, being now in Philadelphia, and left a little daughter of six at Mount Vernon. Beaudoin ventured that the little girl must be deeply upset that she would never see her father again; she answered, *Oh! sir, I am very glad, because he is free now.* The general's house servants are mulattoes, some of whom have kinky hair still but skins as light as ours. I noticed one small boy whose hair and skin were so like our own that if I had not been told, I should never have suspected his ancestry. He is nevertheless a slave for the rest of his life.

We left Mount Vernon the 9th. The general was kind enough to give us letters, and some comments in his own hand on our proposed itinerary.

1. GW's final slave list, taken in the summer of 1799, named 317 people, including 40 whom he hired.

2. Inalienable status.

3. That is, Virginia.

4. Beaudoin served as Louis-Philippe's personal valet.

5. Louis-Philippe's comment reveals that the slaves at Mount Vernon were well aware of the recent, violent slave uprising in the French Caribbean.

1798

ACUTE OBSERVATIONS:
FROM DOMESTIC PURSUITS TO CONCERN FOR THE NATION
Julian Ursyn Niemcewicz

Some Europeans who arrived at Mount Vernon celebrated American independence even as they mourned the loss of liberty in their own countries. Among such travelers was Julian Ursyn Niemcewicz, who had resisted the partitioning of his native Poland by neighboring states. For that he was imprisoned in Russia, along with his compatriot Tadeuz Kosciuszko, a hero of the American War for Independence. After their release the two men took passage for the United States, and in June 1798 Niemcewicz spent several days with the Washingtons. His long and unusually detailed account has a melancholy edge.

Niemcewicz saw Mount Vernon at the height of its development. His description of the estate surpasses those of all other eighteenth-century visitors. Here he offers acute observations of slave life and labor, Washington's gristmill, distillery, and fishing operation, as well as the plantation burial ground. Niemcewicz also reports on his host's passionate concerns about Napoleonic France.

This traveler's account, reprinted from Julian Ursyn Niemcewicz, *Under Their Vine and Fig Tree: Travels through America in 1797–1799, 1805, with Some*

Further Account of Life in New Jersey, translated and edited by Metchie J. E. Budka (Elizabeth, N.J., 1965), 95–108, is in the Collections of the New Jersey Historical Society and is used with permission.

2 June. Mount Vernon. After many distractions and delays, at about eleven o'clock we set out for Mount Vernon. We crossed the river by ferry and followed the Maryland bank. From there Federal City or rather the land destined for the city rises in an amphitheatre. After having made 4 to 5 miles we arrived at the point opposite Alexandria; I saw there an immense field covered with the most beautiful wheat that one could wish for. I asked the reason for this fertility almost unknown in America and very rare in any country. I was told that the ground was fertilized with herrings; that is to say, with the heads and the entrails of this fish. We took 25 minutes to cross the Potwomak once again. I stopped in Alexandria at the merchant's Atkins to buy a pound of cut tobacco. It sells at a dollar a pound, which is excessive for a country which is the fatherland of all tobaccos. While paying I muttered against this costly habit, unclean and unhealthy, but it is not at such a time, bereft of all pleasures, that I could bring myself to renounce it.

We continued through a country scored with ravines and well wooded. After 7 miles of road we arrived at the foot of a hill where the properties of G[enera]l Washington begin. We took a road newly cut through a forest of oaks. Soon we discovered still another hill at the top of which stood a rather spacious house, surmounted by a small cupola, with mezzanines and with blinds painted in green. It is surrounded by a ditch in brick with very pretty little turrets at the corners; these are nothing but outhouses.[1] Two bowling greens, a circular one very near the house, the other very large and irregular, form the courtyard in front of the house. All kinds of trees, bushes, flowering plants, ornament the two sides of the court. Near the two ends of the house are planted two groves of acacia, called here *locust,* a charming tree, with a smooth trunk and without branches leaving a clear and open space for the movement of its small and trembling leaves. The ground where they are planted is a green carpet of the most beautiful velvet. This tree keeps off all kinds of insects. There were also a few catalpa and tulip trees there etc.

We entered into the house. Gl. Washington was at his farm. Madame appeared after a few minutes, welcomed us most graciously and had *punch* served. At two o'clock the Gl. arrived mounted on a gray horse. He shook our hand, dismounted, gave a cut of the whip to his horse which went off by itself to the stable. We chatted a little; then he went off to dress and we to see the interior of the house.

One enters into a hall which divides the house into two and leads to the *piazza*. It is decorated with a few engravings of Claude Lorraine. A kind of small crystal lantern contains the actual key of the Bastille. This relic of despotism was sent to the Gl. by the Marquis de La Fayette. Underneath is a drawing representing the demolition of this formidable castle. Furthermore on the *piazza* one sees a model of it, wholly of a stone which was part of the Bastille; it is a foot and a half high, made with the greatest detail and exactness. It is a pity that the children have already damaged it a little. At the right, on entering, is a *parlor*. One sees there the portrait of Gl. Washington when he was still in the English service, in a blue uniform, red vest and breeches, the whole trimmed with narrow silver braid, and a small hat in the shape of a mushroom. He is represented in the attitude of an officer on the march; lest there should be any doubt he takes out of the pocket of his vest a paper on which is written *March order.* He has a gun slung across his back and a violet sash over his shoulders. Mrs. Washington (née Dandridge), which makes the pair, has a blue gown with her hair dressed a half an inch high and her ears uncovered. In her right hand she carries a flower. This portrait, which was never good, is in addition badly damaged. [There is] a picture representing the family of the Mar[quis] de La Fayette: The Mar[quis] in an American uniform is presenting to his wife, who is seated, his son aged 4 also in an American uniform; his two daughters nearly the same age complete the group. The picture is well painted and well composed but the paint has fallen off in many places. The marquise has a broad slash the whole length of the left side of her face, a slash which has deprived her of an eye; the older of the girls is also one-eyed, and the younger has lost the end of her nose. There is a portrait of the son and daughter of Mrs. Washington by her first marriage: the child is only 5 years old. He is dressed in a suit with a purse, carrying on his fist a red bird. There are portraits in pastel of the Gl., of Madame, of the young Custis, of young La Fayette, and the divine Miss Custis with her hair blown by a storm. An allegorical picture in enamel in honor of the Gl. Two pictures embroidered in faultless needlework, etc., etc.

From this room one goes into a large salon that the Gl. has recently added. It is the most magnificent room in the house. The chimneypiece is in white marble, with beautiful bas-reliefs. A few pictures, engravings after Thrumbull, representing the death of Gl. Warren and of Gl. Montgomery.[2] At the side of the first room is yet another *parlor,* decorated with beautiful engravings representing storms and seascapes. One sees there a superb harpsichord of Miss Custis. On the other side of the hall are the dining room, a bedroom and the library of the Gl; above, several apartments for Madame, Miss Custis and guests. They are all very neatly and prettily furnished.

On the side opposite the front is an immense open portico supported by eight pillars. It is from there that one looks out on perhaps the most beautiful view in the world. One sees there the waters of the Potowmak rolling majestically over a distance of 4 to 5 miles. Boats which go to and fro make a picture of unceasing motion. A lawn of the most beautiful green leads to a steep slope, covered as far as the bank by a very thick wood where formerly there were deer and roebuck, but a short time ago

Charles Willson Peale's 1772 portrait of George Washington shows him in the
uniform of a colonel in the Seven Years' War (1756-63), during which he commanded
provincial troops known as the Virginia Regiment. This is the first known image
of Washington taken from life. (Washington-Custis-Lee Collection, courtesy
of Washington and Lee University, Lexington, Va.)

73

they broke the enclosure and escaped. [There are] robins, blue titmice, Baltimore bird, *the black, red and gold bird.* It is there that in the afternoon and evening the Gl., his family and the *gustes* [guests] go to sit and enjoy the fine weather and the beautiful view. I enjoyed it more than anyone. I found the situation of Mount Vernon from this side very similar to that of Pulawy.[3] The opposite bank, the course of the river, the dense woods all combined to enhance this sweet illusion. What a remembrance!

About three o'clock a carriage drawn by two horses, a young man on horseback alongside, pulled up. A young woman of the greatest beauty[4] accompanied by another who was not beautiful at all. This was one of those celestial figures that nature produces only rarely, that the inspiration of painters has sometimes divined and that one cannot see without ecstasy. Her sweetness is equal to her beauty, and this being, so perfect of form, possesses all the talents: she plays the harpsichord, sings, draws better than any woman in America or even in Europe.

After dinner one goes out onto the portico to read the newspaper. In the evening Gl. Wash[ington] showed us his garden. It is well cultivated and neatly kept; the gardener is an Englishman. One sees there all the vegetables for the kitchen, *Corrents, Rasberys, Strawberys, Gusberys,* quantities of peaches and cherries, much inferior to ours, which the *robins, blackbirds* and Negroes devour before they are ripe.

Opium, some poppies. . . .

One sees also in the garden lilies, roses, pinks, etc. The path which runs all around the bowling green is planted with a thousand kinds of trees, plants and bushes; crowning them are two immense Spanish chestnuts that Gl. Wash[ington] planted himself; they are very bushy and of the greatest beauty. The tree of the *tulip,* called here *Poplar,* or *Tulip Tree,* is very high with a beautiful leaf and the flower in a bell resembling a *Tulip,* white with a touch of orange at the base. The magnolia [is] a charming tree (this tree in South Carolina grows as high as

70 feet and perfumes the forests) with a whitish and smooth trunk; the leaf resembles that of the orange; in bud the flower is like a white acorn which opens out and gives off an odor less strong than the orange but just as agreeable; the fruit is a little cone with crimson seeds; these seeds are held to the cone by small threads. The *Sweet Scented Shroub,* a shrub which grows in a thicket, with a very deep purple, nearly black flower, has a fragrance which from my point of view surpasses all the others: it is an essence of strawberries and pineapple mixed together. The superb catalpa was not yet in flower. The fir of Nova Scotia, *Spruce Tree,* is of a beautiful deep green; it is from their cones that the essence of *Spruce* is extracted to mix it with the beer. [There was] a tree bearing thousands and thousands of pods like little pea pods. A thousand other bushes, for the most part species of laurel and thorn, all covered with flowers of different colors, all planted in a manner to produce the most beautiful hues. The weeping willows were deprived of their greatest beauty. Last winter there was such a great amount of snow that their branches, not being able to support it, broke. Instead of their floating crown these trees appeared like close-cropped whiskbrooms, which did not become them at all. In a word the garden, the plantations, the house, the whole upkeep, proves that a man born with natural taste can divine the beautiful without having seen the model. The Gl. has never left America. After seeing his house and his gardens one would say that he had seen the most beautiful examples in England of this style.

As the sun was setting, we saw the herd returning home. On the lead was a superb bull of English breeding, for which the Gl. paid 200 doll. We then went to see the asses. Mar[quis] de La Fayette sent to him a stallion from Malta and one from Spain with their females. They are large and handsome of their kind. The Gl. keeps up to 50 mules; these crossbred animals are excellent for work and burdens. The asses service the mares and the jennies of the neighbors at a charge of ten dollars per season; for each female, as she is then on board, a half doll. per week is paid for her feed, which is a little dear, and besides this a ½ doll. for the boy.

3 June. The next day, which was Sunday, the Gl. retired to write letters, this day being set aside for this activity. I went out for a walk with Mr. Law.[5] He showed me a hill covered with old chestnuts, oaks, weeping willows, cedars, etc. It was a burial ground. It is there that the inhabitants of Mount Vernon, their eyelids once closed, sleep a peaceful and eternal sleep. Mr. Law was present at the interment of Mrs. Liard who brought up the granddaughters of Mrs. Washington. The ceremony took place in the evening of a beautiful day in Autumn. The sun was setting behind the bluish hills and thick forests of oaks and laurel, its rays falling obliquely on the smooth waters of the Potowmak. A light wind ruffled the leaves of the trees, already half-green and half-yellow. A pastor, a venerable figure with white hair, read the prayer for the dead while the assembled family, the young women with bowed heads, eyes in tears, observed a heavy silence. "I have never seen," he told me, "a more affecting and more august sight."

About one o'clock we had the pleasure of seeing Mrs. Law arrive with her little daughter and then a *gentilman* farmer of the neighborhood with his stout and red-haired wife who had a belt with a buckle of Bohemian Glass. In the evening no music, not even a game of chess; it was Sunday; everyone retired at nine o'clock.

4 June. His Fortune. We left on horseback with Mr. Law to see the Gl.'s farm. Mount Vernon was already a large property when Gl. Washington inherited it from his half brother of the first marriage. When he married Mrs. Custis, he took with her as dowry 20,000 pounds of the money of Virginia, about 70,000 doll. He bought, with a large part of this money, lands at 20 and 30 sh[il]lings per acre, between 4 and 5 pounds (today he would not give them up for ten times as much). His lands in Mount Vernon today enclose 10,000 acres in a single unit. . . .

This morning we saw vast fields covered with different kinds of grain. One hundred acres in peas alone, much rye which is distilled into *whiski*, maize, wheat, flax, large meadows sown to lucerne; the soil although for the most part clayey produces, as a result of good cultivation, abundant harvests. All these lands are divided into four farms with a number of Blacks attached to each and a Black overseer over them. The whole is under the supervision of Mr. Anderson, a Scottish farmer.[6]

We saw a very large mill built in stone. An American machine invented by Evens (who has published a work on mills) for the aeration of the flour is very ingenious. Beside the different kinds of grain that are ground for the use of the house, and for the nourishment of the Blacks, each year a thousand kegs of wheat flour are ground for export. A *boushel* of grain makes a *boushel* of flour; 5 *boushels* are necessary for a barrel. The lowest price being 5 doll. that makes 5,000 doll. per year. Outsiders who come to grind at the mill pay an eighth in kind.

Just near by is a *whiski* distillery. Under the supervision of the son of Mr. Anderson, they distill up to 12 thousand gallons a year (they can distill 50 gallons per day if the weather is not too hot); each gallon at 4 Virginia shilings; that alone should bring in up to 16 thousand doll. I do not know how Mr. Anderson maintains that the distillery produces only 600 pounds. If this distillery produces poison for men, it offers in return the most delicate and the most succulent feed for pigs. They keep 150 of them of the Guinea type, short feet, hollow backs and so excessively bulky that they can hardly drag their big bellies on the ground. Their venerable and corpulent appearance recalled to me our Dominican convents, like so many priors. We saw here and there flocks of sheep. The Gl. has between six and seven hundred. They are not anywhere near as big as those of England. The rose laurel with which the forests abound here is a poison for them and many die of it.

Blacks. We entered one of the huts of the Blacks, for one can not call

After the War for Independence, Washington abandoned tobacco production, Virginia's traditional cash crop, and invested heavily in the cultivation of grains. His gristmill, shown here in a modern photograph (2002), milled wheat, corn, and other grains from Mount Vernon's fields and those of nearby farmers. (Courtesy of the Mount Vernon Ladies' Association)

them by the name of houses. They are more miserable than the most miserable of the cottages of our peasants. The husband and wife sleep on a mean pallet, the children on the ground; a very bad fireplace, some utensils for cooking, but in the middle of this poverty some cups and a teapot. A boy of 15 was lying on the ground, sick, and in terrible convulsions. The Gl. had sent to Alexandria to fetch a doctor. A very small garden planted with vegetables was close by, with 5 or 6 hens, each one leading ten to fifteen chickens. It is the only comfort that is permitted them; for they may not keep either ducks, geese, or pigs. They sell the poultry in Alexandria and procure for themselves a few amenities. They allot them each *one pack* [peck], one gallon of maize per week; this makes one quart a day, and half as much for the children, with 20 herrings each per month. At harvest time those who work in the fields have salt meat; in addition, a jacket and a pair of homespun breeches per year. Not counting women and children the Gl. has 300 Negroes of whom a large number belong to Mrs. Washington. Mr. Anderson told me that there are only a hundred who work in the fields. They work all week, not having a single day for themselves except for holidays. One sees by that that the condition of our peasants is infinitely happier. The mulattoes are ordinarily chosen for servants. According to the laws of Virginia the child follows the condition of the mother; the son or daughter of a mulatto woman and a white is a slave and the issue through the daughter, although white, are still slaves. Gl. Washington treats his slaves far more humanely than do his fellow citizens of Virginia. Most of these gentlemen give to their Blacks only bread, water and blows.

Either from habit, or from natural humor disposed to gaiety, I have never seen the Blacks sad. Last Sunday there were about thirty divided into two groups and playing at prisoner's base. There were jumps and gambols as if they had rested all week. I noticed that all spoke very good English. Why then do the Blacks of the French colonies never speak a good French; rather make a jargon of their own? The reason for it is perhaps that the American masters speak and communicate with them more often than the French who depend entirely for the management of their farms on their overseers who are also black.

5 June. This morning the Gl. had the kindness to go with us on horseback to show us another of his farms. The soil of it was black, much better looking and more fertile than that of the others. We saw two young bulls only one year old of a prodigious size. If the Americans, instead of leaving their herds out to pasture all winter, kept them in the stables, they would be superb, but the opposite prevails, consequently their cows are thin. They prefer to use horses at the plow. The Gl. showed us a plow of his own invention: in the middle on the axle itself is a hollow cylinder filled with grain; this cylinder is pierced with different holes, according to the size of the grain. As the plow moves ahead, the cylinder turns and the grain falls, the ploughshare having prepared the furrow for it, and a little blade behind then covers it with earth. He then took us to see a barn for threshing the grain. It is an octagonal building; on the first story the floor is made from planed poles three inches wide which do not touch, leaving an empty space between. Grain is placed on them and horses, driven at a trot, trample it; the kernels fall through to the bottom. All around the building there are windows for a draft.

I have often heard the Gl. reproached for his reserve and his taciturnity. It is true that he is somewhat reserved in speech, but he does not avoid entering into conversation when one furnishes him with a subject. We spoke of the French Revolution, and these were his words, "The acts of the French, that which they do in Holland, in Italy, and in Switzerland, ought to warn all nations of their intentions; ought to teach them that it is not freedom nor the happiness of men, but an untrammelled ambition and a desire to spread their conquests and to rule everywhere which is the only goal of their measures!"

Washington designed a unique sixteen-sided threshing barn that was built in
the early 1790s on his Dogue Run Farm, part of the estate (see the map on p. 35).
Horses were led up the ramp and into the room where they treaded wheat,
separating grain from chaff, which then fell through spaces between the floor
boards to a storage area below. This labor-saving design was one of many
agricultural innovations that Washington introduced at Mount Vernon and
that earned him a reputation for being the best farmer in the new nation. Near
the barn stood stables for the horses and corn sheds. (Photograph of the
reconstructed complex, 1996, courtesy of the Mount Vernon Ladies' Association)

At the table after the departure of the ladies, or else in the evening
seated under the portico, he often talked with me for hours at a time. His
favorite subject is agriculture, but he answered with kindness all questions that I put to him on the Revolution, the armies, etc. He has a prodigious memory. One time in the evening he listed all the rivers, lakes,

creeks, and the means to procure a communication between these waters from Portsmouth in the province of Maine as far as the Mississippi. This man may have erred during his administration; he may not be exempt from a few faults connected more with his age than with his heart, but in all he is a great man whose virtues equal the services that he has rendered his Fatherland. He has shown courage and talent in combat, perseverance and steadfastness during reverses and difficulties, disinterestedness, having at all times served without reward, and in the time of general enthusiasm of a grateful nation he never wished to accept the slightest recompense. Finally he has shown that he was not eager for glory, for being able to remain all his life at the head of the government he resigned voluntarily from the office of President. The device that he has taken for his arms is very appropriate for him, *exitus acta probat*.[7]

Since his retirement he has led a quiet and regular life. He gets up at 5 o'clock in the morning, reads or writes until seven. He breakfasts on tea and *caks* made from maize; because of his teeth he makes slices spread with butter and honey. He then immediately goes on horseback to see the work in the fields; sometimes in the middle of a field he holds a council of war with Mr. Anderson. He returns at two o'clock, dresses, goes to dinner. If there are guests, he loves to chat after dinner with a glass of Madeira in his hand. After dinner he diligently reads the newspapers, of which he receives about ten of different kinds. He answers letters, etc. Tea at 7 o'clock; he chats until nine, and then he goes to bed.

Mrs. Washington is one of the most estimable persons that one could know, good, sweet, and extremely polite. She loves to talk and talks very well about times past. She told me she remembered the time when there was only one single carriage in all of Virginia. Ladies invited to an entertainment arrived on horseback. All the trade consisted in the little tobacco that was exported. The correspondents in England did not fail to send to their friends one or two pounds of tea, which was a very great present.

I was not as a stranger but a member of the family in this estimable house. They took care of me, of my linen, of my clothes, etc. Mrs. Washington was born on the North river; her maiden name is Dandridge.

6 June. The 6th Mr. Law left for Baltimore. Mrs. Stuart, daughter-in-law of Mrs. Wash[ington],[8] with four of her daughters by her second marriage and her husband arrived in a coach and four with two postillions, and two men on horseback, all black.

7 [June.] I took a long walk on foot to the herring fisheries. They fish for them in April; they have caught as many as 100 thousand of them with a single draw of the net. It is the best nourishment for the Negroes. . . .

8 J[une.] For three years the deer have almost disappeared from the Gl.'s park. When today we discovered three grazing on the grass a little distance from the house, the Gl. suggested to me to look at them close up. We left. He walked very quickly; I could hardly follow him. We maneuvered to force them to leave their retreat and go towards the field, but the maneuver, clever as it was, did not succeed; they plunged into the wood.

9 J[une.] Mrs. Washington made me a gift of a china cup with her monogram and the names of the states of the United States. Miss Custis gave me my monogram in flowers, which she herself has painted very well. . . .

10 [June.] Sunday, cool weather, I caught a river turtle weighing at least 12 pounds. We retired at 9 o'clock.

Blacks. 11 [June.] Monday I had a conversation with Dr. Stuart. He told me: no one knows better than the Virginians the cruelty, inconvenience and the little advantage of having Blacks. Their support costs a great deal; their work is worth little if they are not whipped; the *Surveyor*[9] costs a great deal and steals into the bargain. We would all agree to free these people; but how to do it with such a great number?

They have tried to rent them a piece of land; except for a small number they want neither to work nor to pay their rent. Moreover this unfortunate black color has made such a sharp distinction between the two races. It will always make them a separate caste, which in spite of all the enlightenment of philosophy, will always be regarded as an inferior class which will never mix in the society of Whites. All these difficulties will increase from day to day, for the Blacks multiply. Only a great increase of the population of Whites, a great emigration from Europe, could render this less apparent. . . .

12 [June.] We spoke of the authors who have written the History of the Revolution. Gordon,[10] who has the most details, came to visit the archives of the Gl. They consist of between 30 and 40 cases of papers, containing all the military expeditions, reports, journals, correspondence with Congress, with the Generals, etc. What a wealth of material! However, Gordon stayed only three weeks to read them and extract them. The Gl. intends to build a separate house for the deposit of his archives since the collection has become so voluminous.

Mrs. Washington showed me a small collection of medals struck during the Revolution. There is one of at least 100 ducats in gold, with the head closely resembling that of Gl. Washington, which was struck on the occasion of the evacuation of Boston; one for Gl. Gates for the defeat of Bourgoyne; others for Gl. Green, Gl. Morgan, Col. Howard and Col. Washington on the occasion of the battle of Cowpen; one for Franklin, for M. de Fleury, for Paul Jones; one with the head of Liberty on one side and on the reverse France defending America with her shield against Gr[eat] Britain. Further there is the order of Cincinnatus in diamonds presented by the French Navy; a box in gold, very badly turned, presented by the city of New York with the freedom of the city.

In the evening the General went to the storehouse to look over things which had come from Europe, just as we do when goods come from Gdańsk during the spring floods.

Every day I notice new birds arriving to nest in the peaceful garden of these parts: turtledoves, cardinals all crimson. The Baltimore, orange with black bands, these latter singing very well. They are beautiful; they are magnificent; I would prefer, however, a nightingale from Poland. . . .

June 13. Mr. Law returned from Baltimore. . . .

In the morning we went out with the steward Anderson and some negroes to catch fish. The manner of fishing is similar to ours but the fish are entirely different. When the nets were hauled in, they were reasonably well filled but only with small fish. The largest fish was the *garfish*, nearly two feet in length and rather similar to one that is called in the Mediterranean the *pescespada*. Its skin is as tough as shagreen and mottled with leopard-like spots, a snout six inches long like the beak of a bird, with both lower and upper teeth as sharp as needles. This fish is skinned while still alive. The flesh is red and it is little esteemed, serving only as food for negroes. *Cat Fisch*, so called because it has a head somewhat resembling that of a cat and, when disturbed, it gives out a cat-like cry. It is about a foot long with a very large head in proportion to its length, "whiskers" in four rows, and fins which when touched inflict a painful wound. There are two kinds, white and black. The first is considered excellent, especially for broth; the second, which is black, is left for the blacks. We caught 30 of the latter kind; the hapless negroes got them all. *Tobac[c]o box* is a flat fish five inches in length and practically circular. Its scales are dark green, pierced through with gold; around the head at both sides it has two circles like shilling pieces; half crimson, half black; it is difficult to find anything more lovely. These fish, which are abundant in practically all American rivers, are as good in taste as they are beautiful to behold. There are many perches and silver roaches. River turtles, one foot in length, have a black shell shot through with red. They provide both meat and eggs which are excellent. Finally we caught a crayfish. It was the first which I had seen in America; the inhabitants of these parts hold them in disdain and do not eat them.

On our return we found a notable and unexpected company from Alexandria. The table in the great hall was set out with a Sèvres porcelain service with places for 20. The General, in high spirits, was gracious and full of attention to everybody. Amongst the guests were the young Randolphs; I do not know whether both their ages would add up to 38, and already they are the parents of three children. Mrs. [Fitzhugh], who in corpulence and girth gives way only to the late Semiramis, was in a gay humour and had an enormous appetite. As she swept through one platter after another, her husband laughingly encouraged her with these words: *"Betsy, a little more, a little more."*

In the evening, after the departure of the company the General, sitting with Mr. Law and me under the portico, read to us a letter which he had just received from a friend in Paris. This letter written with sense, dispassion, and with a sound knowledge of the situation in France and the politics of those who rule her, gave us an opportunity for conversation about the wrongs suffered by America at French hands, and about the bloody struggles which might shortly break out between the two countries. This conversation aroused the passionate wrath of the venerable citizen and commander. I have never heard him speak with so much candor nor with such heat.[11]

"Whether," he said, "we consider the injuries and plunder which our commerce is suffering" (up to 50 million dollars) "or the affront to our national independence and dignity in the rejection of our envoys, or whether we think on the oppression, ruin and final destruction of all free people through this military government, everywhere we recognize the need to arm ourselves with a strength and zeal equal to the dangers with which we are threatened. Continued patience and submission will not deliver us, any more than submission delivered Venice or others. Submission is vile. Yea, rather than allowing herself to be insulted to this degree, rather than having her freedom and independence trodden under foot, America, every American, I, though old, will pour out the last drop of blood which is yet in my veins."

"They censure Mr. Adams[12] for haste in deeds and excessive boldness in words; from the moment that I left the administration, I have not written a word to Mr. Adams, nor yet received a word from him except the dispatches which we have seen in the papers; I do not know what are those other sources of information on which he acts; with all this I am certain, as a reasonable and honest person, as a good American, that he cannot do other than he does. I, in his place, perhaps would be less vehement in expression but I would prepare myself steadily and boldly in the same fashion."

The strong and noble feelings of this man pierced my heart with respect and emotion.

June 14. In the evening, for the last time, pretty Miss Custis sang and played on the harpsichord. The next day, after having risen before dawn, I walked now for the last time, about the green groves of Mo[u]nt Vernon. For the last time I looked out on the open view, on the clear and beautiful stream Potowmak. Then at six in the morning with gratitude for the hospitable welcome, and with sorrow silent and unexpressed, I took my leave of the honorable Washington, his worthy wife and the beautiful, good and kind Miss Custis. In company of both Mr. and Mrs. Law and their beautiful *baby* daughter I returned through Alexandria to George Town.

1. Niemcewicz apparently was referring to the brick-enclosed gardens and the garden houses.

2. After some time as an aide-de-camp to GW, John Trumbull of Connecticut studied painting in Europe and by the 1790s was known for his depictions of the American

Revolution. His subjects included Joseph Warren, killed at the Battle of Bunker Hill in 1775, and Richard Montgomery, who died in the American assault on Quebec that same year.

3. A Polish estate.

4. Eleanor Parke Custis.

5. Thomas Law, husband of Eliza Parke Custis.

6. James Anderson assumed the duties of farm manager in early 1797.

7. "The result justifies the deed."

8. Eleanor Calvert Custis, widow of Martha Washington's son John, remarried, to Dr. David Stuart. The couple lived near Mount Vernon.

9. That is, the overseer.

10. The Reverend William Gordon worked at Mount Vernon in 1784 and subsequently published his *History of the Rise, Progress, and Establishment of the Independence of the United States of America: Including an Account of the Late War; and of the Thirteen Colonies, from Their Origin to That Period*, 4 vols. (London, 1788).

11. As the two men spoke, war with Napoleon's regime appeared imminent. For several years French ships had been seizing American merchant vessels on the high seas. Furthermore, when an American delegation arrived to meet with the French government, officials demanded a bribe even to speak with them.

12. John Adams, GW's successor in the presidency.

1799

"Tranquil Happiness Reigns"

Elizabeth Ambler Carrington

More than any other eighteenth-century visitor's observations that survive, those of Elizabeth Ambler Carrington concern female activities at Mount Vernon, including Martha Washington's role as plantation mistress and, second, the birth of Eleanor Parke Custis Lewis's first child. Because Mrs. Carrington was accompanied by her husband Edward Carrington, a Revolutionary War veteran, she also witnessed George Washington in a most convivial mood as the two Virginians traded memories of their military campaigns and talked of compatriots. There was no hint, during the Carringtons' visit in November 1799, that Washington would be dead in less than a month.

This letter to Anne [Nancy] Fisher, 22 and 27 November, appears in "A Visit to Mount Vernon—A Letter of Mrs. Edward Carrington to Her Sister, Mrs. George Fisher," *William and Mary Quarterly,* 2nd ser., 18 (1938): 198–202, and is used with permission.

When near you My Dear Nancy, I have often a great passion to express my feelings in an epistolary way; how can it be wondered then, that now, when more than a hundred miles from you, this propensity should still exist, particularly when seated at a spot of all others best calculated to produce a letter most acceptable to you.

We arrived here on the 20th just in time enough for dinner, after a pleasant journey made more than ordinarily agreeable by a continuation of fine weather which enabled us to make several pleasant calls on friends who are agreeably scattered on the way from Fredericksburg to Alexandria (that is to say if you take the road up the Potomac).

Yes we arrived at this venerable mansion in perfect safety, where we are experiencing every mark of hospitality & kindness that the good old General's continued friendship to Col. C. could lead us to expect; his reception of my husband was that of a Brother; he took us each by the hand & with a warmth of expression not to be described, pressed mine, & told me that I had conferred a favour, never to be forgotten, in bringing his old friend to see him; then bidding a servant to call the ladies entertained us most facetiously till they appeared.

Mrs. W[ashington] venerable, kind & plain, & resembling very much our aunt A——. Mrs. Stewart[1] her daughter-in-law once Mrs. Custis with her two young daughters, Misses S—— all pleasant & agreeable. Mrs. H—— Lewis formerly Miss P——d of Richmond and last, tho' not least Mrs. L. Lewis—but how [to] describe her.[2] Once I had heard my neighbour, Mrs. Tucker give a romantic account of her, when Miss Custis,—now her lovely figure, made doubly interesting by a light fanciful summer dress with a garland of flowers she had just entwined, and an apronfull she had selected, came in to throw them at her grandmama's feet—all which I considered as the fanciful effusions of my friends romantic turn of mind, but now when I see her the Matron, for such her situation makes her appear, though she has only been ten months a wife, lovely as nature could form her, improved in every female accomplishment & what is still more interesting, amiable & obliging in every department that makes woman most charming, particularly in her conduct to her aged Grandmother & the General, whom she always calls Grampa, I seem actually transported in beholding her. Having once seen her as she passed through our Town seems to give me a claim to her kindness, and her attentions are unremitted. On retiring for the night she took me into her apartment which was elegantly prepared for an expected event, & where we separated; "how glad I am that you are here," she said. "What a pleasure it will be to me, to retain you till this dreaded event has passed." I assured her that nothing could give more pleasure than to remain & offer every friendly aid in my power. In this promise I thought this morning I should be indulged, for on entering the breakfast room, I understood she had been complaining all night, but unfortunately my husband spied the armchair carried upstairs, & a moment after ordered our carriage. In vain does the General insist upon our stay, promising to take him over the grounds and farm, & showing him the mill &c &c which will occupy him till 3. But no—the world could not tempt him to stay, at a time, when he said, everyone should leave the family entirely undisturbed, but that after a few days, when we should have finished our visit to our friends in Maryland, we would again see them and prolong our visit. Is it not vexatious to have so scrupulous a husband; nothing could stress me more than to leave that charming family at such a moment but I am bound to obey & at 12 we are to leave this place for Washington; when I return you may expect to hear from me.

27th November. After passing a week most charmingly with my numerous friends in & about the City, we returned to finish our visit to this revered Mansion. . . .

I having missed the post, I continue to scribble on, & am well pleased that my letter was not ready for the post, as I have much to say, & I am really delighted that our first visit here was shortened so that we are at liberty to finish it at a time when our presence is of more consequence to this amiable family than it would [have] been before.

It is really an enjoyment to be here, to witness the tranquil happiness that reigns throughout the house (except now & then a little bustle, occa- sioned by the young squire Custis[3] when he returns from hunting, bring- ing in a *"Valient Deer"* as he terms it, "that Grand Pa & the Col. will devour")—nice venison I assure you it is, & my taste in seasoning the stew is not passed unnoticed while the whole party, I wont say devour it, but do it ample justice.

My mornings are spent charmingly alternately in the different cham- bers; first an hour after breakfast with the lady in the straw—dressing the pretty little stranger, who is the delight of the Grand-Ma;[4] then we repair to the old lady's room, which is precisely on the style of our good old aunt's, that is to say nicely fixed for all sorts of work. On one side sits the chambermaid with her knitting, on the other a little colored pet, learning to sew, an old, decent woman with her table and shears cutting out the negroes winter clothes, while the good old lady directs them all, incessantly knitting herself, & pointing out to me several pair of nice coloured stockings & gloves she had just finished, & presenting me with a pair half done, begs me to finish, & wear for her sake.

Her netting too is a great source of amusement, & is so neatly done, that all the younger part of the family are proud of trimming their dresses with it and have furnished me with a whole suit, so that I shall appear "A la domestique" at the first party we have when we get home.

It is wonderful after a life spent as these good people have necessarily spent theirs to see them in retirement assume domestic manners that prevail in our country, when but a year since they were forced to forego all the innocent delights which are so congenial to their years and tastes, to sacrifice to the parade of the drawing room & the Levee.[5]

The recollection of these last days as Mrs. W—— calls them, seem to fill her with regret, but the extensive knowledge she has gained in this general intercourse with persons from all parts of the world has made her a most interesting companion, & having a vastly retentive memory, she presents an entire history of half a century.

The weather is too wintry to enjoy outdoor scenes but as far as I can judge in a view from the windows, the little painting we have seen that hangs up in my friend Mrs. Wood's drawing room furnishes a good specimen. Everything within doors is neat & elegant, but nothing remarkable, except the paintings of different artists which have been sent as specimens of their talents. I think there are five portraits of the General, some done in Europe, some in America that do honour to the painter. There are other specimens of the fine arts from various parts of the world, that are admirably executed, & furnish pleasant conversation. Besides these there is a complete Green-house which at this season is a vast, a great source of pleasure. Plants from every part of the world seem to flourish in the neatly finished apartment, & from the arrangement of the whole, I conclude that it is managed by a skilful hand but whose I cannot tell. Neither the General nor Mrs. W—— seem more interested in it than the visitors.

We have met with no company here, but are told that scarcely a week passes without some and often more than is comfortable or agreeable.

When transient persons, who call from curiosity, they are treated with civility, but never interfere with the order of the house, or the General's disposition of time, which is as regular as when at the head of the Army or in the President's chair. Even friends who make a point of visiting him are left much to themselves, indeed scarcely see him from breakfast to dinner, unless he engages them in a ride, which is very agreeable to him. But from dinner till tea our time is most charmingly spent. Indeed one evening the General was so fascinating & drew my husband out into so many old stories, relating to several campaigns where they had been much together, & had so many inquiries made respecting their mutual friends, particularly Kosiusko and Pulaski who have always corresponded with Col. C——, whose characters afford great interest that it was long after twelve when we separated.

1. Eleanor Calvert Custis Stuart.

2. Eleanor Parke Custis, granddaughter of Martha Washington, married Lawrence Lewis, son of GW's sister Betty, at Mount Vernon in February 1799. GW gave the couple part of his Mount Vernon lands, on which they subsequently built Woodlawn.

3. George Washington Parke Custis.

4. Eleanor Lewis delivered her child on 27 November.

5. The Washingtons returned home from the presidency in 1797.

1801

DINNER WITH THE WIDOW WASHINGTON
Samuel Latham Mitchill

Although brief, the following letter nonetheless is informative. It reveals a continuing flow of visitors to Mount Vernon in the years just after George Washington's death. Moreover, the letter, from Samuel Latham Mitchill to his wife, refutes what became an oft-repeated characterization of Martha Washington in widowhood: inconsolable after her husband's death, she kept to a small garret room. Mitchill, a respected scientist and literary man, represented New York in Congress.

This letter, dated 7 December, is found in "Dr. Mitchill's Letters from Washington: 1801–1813," *Harper's New Monthly Magazine* 58 (1879): 742.

I rode this morning from Gadsby's Hotel, in Alexandria, on the Virginia side of the Potomac, on a visit to the celebrated estate of Mount Vernon, lately the property and residence of General Washington. . . .

My companions on this visit were Mr. Van Ness and Major Holmes. On our way we met Colonel Walker, Mr. and Mrs. Bayard, of Delaware, and Mr. and Mrs. Lowndes, of South Carolina, returning from a visit to Mount Vernon. On our arrival we were received by Mr. Lewis, a gentle-man who married one of the Misses Custis, a granddaughter of Mrs. Washington, and who, with his wife, now resides here.[1] Presently Mrs. Washington and her other granddaughter, the celebrated Mrs. Law,[2] now here on a visit, entered. The old lady was habited in black, and wore a plain cap with a black ribbon; she was affable and polite, and made us welcome in that hospitable though unceremonious manner that without hesitation we agreed to stay and dine. Mrs. Law was dressed in white, and both looked and acted in that engaging and superior way for which she is so justly famed. Her little daughter and her husband were with her. Three young ladies, the Misses Stewart and a Miss Henly, and Mrs. Washington's grandson, Mr. Custis, also joined us a little before dinner. Mrs. Washington presided like a lady of hospitality and good sense, tem-pered by much acquaintance with company. Every thing was neat and well-ordered, bespeaking her to be quite the mistress of her household, and regulating all its concerns.

1. Lawrence Lewis and his wife lived at Mount Vernon until their Woodlawn house was completed.
2. Eliza Parke Custis Law.

1802

Mount Vernon during Martha Washington's Last Days

Thomas Pim Cope

When people no longer could visit Mount Vernon to see the living
Washington, they came to venerate his accomplishments and character
and to experience—visually and tactilely—his domestic world. In May
1802 the Philadelphia merchant Thomas Pim Cope was among the first
to describe in writing what soon became a popular ritual, a pilgrimage
of homage, mourning, and remembrance. Subjects he committed to his
diary—the condition of the road from Alexandria to Mount Vernon, the
tomb, the appearance of the first floor of the mansion, including a key to
the Bastille mounted on a wall—subsequently were mentioned in numer-
ous other eyewitness accounts. This account is also the first to mention
evident decline of the estate's agricultural operations.

This diary excerpt is in the Quaker Collection, Haverford College Library, Haverford, Pa., and is used with permission.

[May] 20th[.] This morning has been taken up in a visit to mount vernon, wither we have been accompanied by B. Dearborn & Jno. G. Lad, a merchant of Alexandria. We left our Inn at 8 & arrived in about an hour & an half. The road like all which we have seen in this country, is rough, & badly attended, tho a small part is pretended to be a turnpike, & if large holes of mud & water in the centre & deep ruts, & sidling banks be the true indications of a turnpike, then this deserves the name. A few negro huts & their ragged inhabitants, a small number of cultivated fields, bearing miserable crops of wheat & rye, and forests of crooked knotty timber, were the principal objects that saluted our eyes as we passed this dreary road, until we came in view of Mount Vernon which suddenly bursts upon the sight at the distance of half a mile from the mansion as you emerge from a thick wood. The river is not seen after leaving the high grounds back of Alexandria till it is met with in front of the house, a space of between 8 & 9 miles by land.

The pleasure which we had anticipated in this visit was greatly diminished by the illness of Lady Washington. She is confined to her bed, & from the account given of her by Doctor Craik,[1] the family physician, has not many days to survive. This gentleman received us with attention, conversed sensibly & affably, & politely conducted us round the premises. He evinced a disposition to render our visit as agreeable to us as circumstances would admit.

Doctor Craik is 74 years of age, & resides in Alexandria. he was sent for on the first indisposition of Lady Washington, & has remain'd at Mount Vernon ever since, as she will not consent to his leaving her. She has been sick for a fortnight. He was the old friend and companion of her late illustrious husband & served with him in Braddock[']s army. This venerable physician was with the General in his dying moments, & supported him in his arms as he expired. He spoke of this circumstance with tender emotion, & of the character of his departed friend with high veneration. His respect for the widow is little less enthusiastic. He tells me that she is advanced of 70 & has never left home since the death of the General. Her time is spent principally in domestic cares. She is very industrious, & fond of reading & knitting. To visitants she is affable, hospitable & attentive. The death of her husband affected her very sensibly. She has not entered either his study or the apartment in which he died since the removal of his corps, nor can any entreaty induce her to change the lodging room which she then selected for herself in the attic story immediately under the roof, & which is a small inconvenient uncomfortable apartment. She now promises Doctor Craik that should she recover from the present attack, she will consent to lodge in some other part of the house more airy & commodious, but of this there is little probability, as her health has been wasting for the last twelve months, & yesterday a chilly fit deprived her, during the paroxysm, of the power of speech. he thinks another must deprive her of life.

The mansion at Mount Vernon stands on a high bank on the west side of the Potomac, about gun shot from the river, & the ground in the rear also falls away to a considerable distance, so that from the moment it is seen as you advance towards it by land, it is a very conspicuous object. the intermediate space is little better than a barren heath, on which cinquefoil finds a scanty vegetation. here & there a small copse of trees relieve the eye & animate the scene.

The building itself is 2 stories high, 25 feet deep & between 80 & 90 in front or length. It is a frame, & rough cast so as to resemble white freestone, & is decorated with a cupalo. near at hand are several small buildings for accommodation of the negros &c. two of these, one of which is used as a kitchen, are connected with the main building by means of open piazzas. as these wings fall back, & the connecting piazzas are curved, the whole taken together forms an irregular segment of a circle. The stabling stands aloof, & has nothing in its appearance very neat or remarkable. in the barnyard, which is not very clean, we saw several scrubby cows & oxen, whose lank sides bespoke the leanness of their pasture. a circular haha[2] encompasses about 6 acres of ground directly back of the mansion. the disposition of this ground is judicious & extremely pleasing. thro the centre runs a broad avenue from the mansion to the opposite border, swelling about the middle so as to occupy about 3 acres of the whole enclosure. This is a most delightful lawn, on which they are now making a rich crop of hay. It is through this avenue that the house is seen from the westward. On the right & left are the gardens, containing a good collection of trees, shrubs, flowers, and garden vegetables, exotic & domestic. The fruit trees are well charged, & consist of a considerable variety. Some of the cherries are red & nearly ripe. A small grove of native cedars shelters the kitchen garden from the west & nw winds, & also several fine looking fig trees, which thus protected make a grateful return of excellent fruit. The gardens are attended by a negro, & are in neat flourishing condition.

From the front of the house, which is graced with a broad portico extending the entire length of the building, supported by square pillars & paved with flag[stone] neatly set, there is an extensive view of the broad smooth surface of the Potomac & its bold undulated gravelly shores. There is a grassy slope for several rods from the house towards the river, terminated by a thicket of brush & small trees, which was formerly occupied as a park.[3] Just within the upper margin of this thicket the remains of the General are deposited in the family vault. I approached this humble recepticle of the once illustrious chieftain, with reverential respect. it was an awful involuntary sentiment, inspired by the solemn recollection, that it contained the mouldering corpse of the greatest man on earth, a loathsome carcase, which, when animated with the etherial fire of Washington, was the love, the admiration, the dread of nations. Peace to the spirit of the mighty dead. May thy soul, oh Washington, find, in heaven, a just & sure recompence for thy great services on earth, & rest, forever, in the bosom of thy father & thy God.

The entrance to the vault is closed with a rude oaken low door, raised perpendicularly on the side of the hill. a few bricks crumbling into ruin, support the casement, on which these lines are written with a pencil.

Columbia groans beneath the dreadful wound,
And Europe echoes to the mournful sound.
The sons of freedom shudder at the stroke,
And universal virtue feels the shock.

To those I added the following lines from Gray[']s inimitable Elegy.

The pomp of heraldry, the boast of power.
And all that beauty, all that wealth e'er gave,
Await alike the inevitable hour;
The paths of glory lead but to the grave.

The top of the vault is over grown with low cedars, & is not distinguishable from the rest of the bank into which it is inserted. Our small company remained for a considerable time as if rivetted to this spot. One placed himself on the green turf & mused, with his head resting on his arms. Another stood alone among the thicket with folded arms & down cast eyes. A third reclined against a tree & wept. For a time none ventured to break the deep silence of the place, & when utterence came, it was in the form of a whisper. There was nothing artificial in this, nothing premeditated. All was the effect of nature & the offspring of the moment. After this involuntary pause, we returned to the mansion.

We were conducted into several of the apartments, in all of which we discerned simplicity, neatness & taste. The building & style of finishing is quite plain. There are few architectural ornaments about it. Considering that it is the produce of patchwork, it preserves more uniformity than is common in like cases. It was an old family residence, & the General has from time to time made such additions & improvements as occasion required. Yet on the whole it is a slight building, neither is the furniture uncommonly rich or elegant. it has rather a comfortable, substantial appearance, not void of fashion or taste. The drawing room which is probably about 24 feet square, & the largest in the house, is hung round with a number of paintings & engravings of good workmanship. . . .

The mantel in this room is an elegant piece of work. Two fluted columns of a reddish cast & veiny support a large slab of the most beau-

EXPERIENCING MOUNT VERNON | 1802

tiful white Italian marble, on which the chissel of the artist has placed several figures representing an evening view of a farm yard. The centre groupe consists of oxen, sheep & lambs, driven by a woman & a little boy. At a small distance another woman has drawn some water from a well, & is in the act of pouring it from the bucket into a tub, probably to water the flock. Another & not the least interesting is a boy returned from ploughing. he has just loosened his wearied horse from the plough, while his faithful dog sits gazing at him. The hearth is of chequered marble in small pieces & suitable to the rest. A grate is fixed in the fire place for burning coal, with which Virginia abounds. It has become a very common fuel in this country, so far as I have observed.

In the hall a key of the bastile is carefully preserved in a glass case. It is one solid piece of Iron with a handle of the barrel form, & not larger than is usually found in front door locks.

The other apartments contain a number of engravings & paintings. The likeness of the general & his wife in younger life, of her children, & of several persons of distinction, were observed. but none of these rooms are as expensively furnished as the drawing room, & in general it may be said of the furniture, chairs, carpets, hangings &c that they have seen their best days.

In the portico were several species of the parrot. among the rest a cockatoo, who on seeing Polly seated left his cage with a quick pace and endeavoured to gain her favour by a familiarity which thwarted his design. For alarmed at the hurried motion & chattering of the poor fellow, she fled & left him as destitute as before. The doctor observed to us that this bird was the favourite of Lady Washington, who fed & caressed him daily, & being neglected since her sickness he seemed quite lost & dejected.

I conversed with the steward or manager of the farm. The whole tract

Many visitors sought out this key to the Bastille prison, whose destruction
in 1789 touched off the French Revolution. Lafayette sent the key to Washington,
and it hangs in the central hallway of the mansion. Benson J. Lossing, a prolific
nineteenth-century historian and journalist, drew this sketch for inclusion in his book
Mount Vernon and Its Associations: Historical, Biographical, and Pictorial (1859).
(Courtesy of Special Collections, University of Virginia Library)

is said to consist of 8 or 10 thousand acres. of these one thousand only
are under tillage. The best parts are higher up the river & produce from
5 to 7½ bushels of wheat pr acre. last year they sold 2,700 bushels, & this
was mentioned in a way which induces me to suppose it was considered
as a good years production. General Washington was esteemed to be a
good practical farmer. it is therefore probable that his lands are in as high
a state of cultivation & improvement as any in the neighbourhood, & yet
this is a scanty crop for so extensive a farm. . . .

Altho the untoward situation of the family cut us off from a large portion of our enjoyments, yet I experienced something of a melancholy satisfaction in this trip, which I should find it very difficult to describe. I would not divest myself of the conscious recollection that this had lately been the seat of the great Washington, that on these very grounds he trod ten thousand times before me, & that it still contained the cold remains of that matchless man. . . .

We retraced the same dull road on our return, but with different feelings. . . .

[May] 25th[.] The public paper announces the final exit of Martha Washington. She died on the 22d. two days after I was at Mount Vernon.

1. Dr. James Craik, veteran of both the Seven Years' War and the War for Independence, acted as physician to the Washington household, including slaves.
2. The low-lying walls, called ha-has, kept animals at a distance from the house.
3. GW's deer park.

1818

"INGRATITUDE IS UPON US"
A Letter to a Friend in Richmond

Upon Martha Washington's death in 1802, Bushrod Washington, a nephew of the general and a Supreme Court justice, inherited four thousand acres of the estate. He and his wife, Julia Ann Blackburn Washington, made it their home until they died within days of each other in 1829. During those years a new genre of writing about Mount Vernon developed, and it persisted through the Civil War. In addition

to recording their experiences in diaries and personal correspondence,
some visitors now published accounts in newspapers and magazines,
thereby bringing detailed knowledge of the site to large public audiences.
Furthermore, these narratives often included, in addition to the writers'
experiences, assertions of Mount Vernon's importance to the nation and
opinions about what should or should not be done there.

The following letter is an early, forceful example of the new genre.
Upset that not even a plaque identified the old family tomb in which
Washington was interred, the unknown writer took to the pages of the
National Intelligencer, *published in the District of Columbia, to summon*
citizens to action. The letter also makes clear that, at a time when steam-
boat travel made the site accessible to large groups of people, Mount
Vernon nonetheless was imagined as a place apart from the bustling
world beyond its borders.

This letter is found in "Tomb of Washington," *National Intelligencer*
(Washington, D.C.), 19 Dec. 1818.

I am invited to visit the tomb of Washington tomorrow, in the steam boat
Washington, with ladies and gentlemen, members of Congress, and old
revolutionary officers. I shall here stop my letter until I return, when I
will complete it.

On yesterday morning we went on board of the steam boat *Washington* with about forty or fifty ladies and gentlemen. We carried with us
that excellent band of marine music. The moment the boat moved, the
band played Washington's march: on passing Alexandria, we were
cheered by the shipping; and, on passing down the Potomac, we landed
on the left bank at Fort Washington,[1] and were received in a very handsome style, by Col. Roger Jones, commandant there, and the Inspector,
General Wool. . . . The garrison performed several evolutions. They

appeared to be a body of fine looking men, and should the enemy visit the fort again, they will meet with a hearty reception.

We next moved for Mount Vernon, and soon that beautiful promontory appeared to the view, on the Virginia shore. It commands a prospect of all the surrounding country. The steam boat could not get in less than a quarter of a mile of the shore; we were, therefore, obliged to be conveyed in a small boat. I was among the last that landed, the consequence of which was, that the company were returning from the tomb before I came up with them. I understood, while there, they were deeply affected. I joined them all at the houses of Mount Vernon, and after viewing the green house, the beautiful shrubbery where every one was desirous of taking the smallest relic, if it were but a leaf, or bit of the bark of the trees, the company next went on to the boat again, and as it was some time before they could get on board, I went with a gentleman to view the tomb at leisure. It is situated on the declivity of the river hill, and over it is a mound of earth, with trees growing on its sides, and on the top. It has a plain door. Here I lingered the last of the company; and when I had paid my devotion to the tomb, my heart was smitten when I reflected I had been on a party of pleasure to the city of Washington, admiring the rising glory of my country, and its government, while here laid the hero, the patriot, and the immortal Washington, who had achieved its liberty and independence, and who had contributed more than any earthly being to its happiness and aggrandizement; the father and saviour of his country, and who was permitted to remain in obscurity and neglect, without a mausoleum, monument, inscription, a stone, or any thing else to point [where] the hero and statesman repose or any evidence of his country's gratitude. The idea of ingratitude, rushing on my mind, was gall and wormwood to my heart. I had seen General Washington twenty-five years ago, in the city of Richmond, on his tour to the south, when

President of the United States; the admiration of the world, and the adoration of his country; the most accomplished hero, patriot, statesman, and gentleman that ever lived, and I found him here buried on his own estate; and that his country had not expended one single cent for even a tomb stone!

Every thing great and good in America is called Washington; its capitol, its cities, towns, counties, and districts, all bear his name; the world is filled with the renown and splendor of his arms and virtues; but here is no mark, no inscription, not even a stone to tell where Washington lies; the savior of his country, like the savior of the world, could say, "this people honoreth me with their lips, but their hearts are far from me"— or they would honor him in death, as well as in life. My mind was so forcibly affected on this occasion, that I declared, on my return to Washington, I would tell it to the people of the United States, publish it in the streets of Washington to Congress, and particularly their predecessors, how cruelly they had neglected the remains of their once beloved Washington; and I am confident, if the people of the United States could see how they are disposed of, they would instantly compel Congress to do something that would wash out the stain of ingratitude, which, if not quickly removed, will become fixed, and forever remain an indelible stain and disgrace to the nation.

I was viewing, a few days since, at the capitol, in Washington, the statue of the 'genius of liberty,' &c. forming under the hands of an excellent artist from Italy, for the purpose of ornamenting the hall of the House of Representatives, &c. But I wished to see the statue of General George Washington, which would not only be the most appropriate ornament for the capitol of Washington, but the delight of America, the admiration of the world: but there was none. I could exclaim, like the stranger described by a writer of feeling, on a visit to the city of Washington—

John Gadsby Chapman, a Virginian who studied art in Europe, returned to his native state and about 1833 produced several paintings showing Mount Vernon at that time, including this view of the family tomb. The simple vault in which George and Martha Washington originally were interred stunned some visitors, who thought it bespoke Americans' neglect to honor the hero of the Revolution sufficiently, whereas others considered it a symbolically appropriate resting place for the man who had returned from war, and later the presidency, to lead the life of citizen-farmer. (Courtesy of the Homeland Foundation, Inc., Amenia, N.Y.)

"Shew me the statue of your Washington, that I may contemplate the majestic form that encompassed his mighty soul; that I may gaze on those features once lightened up by every virtue; that I may learn to love virtue as I behold them. Alas! there is no such statue. Lead me then, Americans, to the tomb your country has provided for her deliverer—to the everlasting monument they have erected to his fame." His grave is in the bosom of his own sod, and the cedar that was watered by his own hand, is all that rests on it. Tell me, whence is this inhumanity and supineness; is it envy, jealousy, or ingratitude? Or is it, that, in the great struggle for power and place, every thing is forgotten, every noble, generous, national sentiment is disregarded & despised? Whatever be the cause of it, ingratitude is upon us, until it be removed. The former representatives of the people are to blame, and not the people themselves; altho' they suffer for the neglect of congress. It is true that Congress some years past proposed to build a monument at Washington city, provided Judge Washington would consent to the removal of his uncle there; but Judge Washington could not, with propriety, consent to the proposition, it being the will and desire of Gen. Washington that he should be buried at Mount Vernon.[2] Now, under all circumstances, as Congress could not, with propriety, get the remains of Gen. Washington removed to Washington City, they ought to have erected a monument at Mount Vernon—not to the clouds, but a plain and neat one, pointing to Heaven, where his spirit has certainly gone. Mount Vernon, in my humble opinion, is the most proper place, on earth, under all circumstances, for the erection of the monument; and from the favorable opinion I entertain of the present Congress, it is hoped something will be done, the present session, on the occasion. On my return, I stated to all the members with whom I had the honor of an acquaintance, what I had seen and felt on this occasion. I went to Congress Hall, on the next day, and saw members rise to make motions, and for the first time in my life wished sincerely that I was a Member of that honorable body, only that I might move a resolution, that something might be done relative to the tomb of Washington. After my return from the tomb, Congress had no charms for me; I soon left the hall, came to my room, and determined that I would return home the next day; and derived great consolation when I thought I should once more see Mount Vernon, where I shall leave my heart.

1. Fort Washington stands on a bluff on the Maryland side of the Potomac River, northeast of Mount Vernon. It fulfilled part of GW's vision for the development of the Potomac and its headwaters, namely as a federal fort guarding the entrance to the new capital city, a few miles upriver. However, when British troops attacked Washington, D.C., during the War of 1812, they landed farther east and marched overland across Maryland. Rather than allow the British to occupy the fort, its American defenders destroyed it. After the war it was rebuilt.

2. Congress in 1816 asked BW for permission to remove the remains of GW and Martha Washington to the nation's capital. BW refused, citing his uncle's explicit instructions to be interred at Mount Vernon.

1821
SOLD: FIFTY-FOUR NEGROES
Bushrod Washington

Bushrod Washington was the first heir to Mount Vernon—but not the last—to receive public rebuke for the way he managed the estate. As the episode related here dramatically demonstrates, the site stood apart from the rest of the United States only in imagination, not reality. After visitors with strong antislavery feelings allegedly told some of Judge Washington's slaves that they would automatically be freed at their master's death, his response suggests fear for his life: he sold fifty-four African Americans, more than half of the black population at Mount Vernon.

That was in August 1821. A Leesburg, Virginia, newspaper, the Genius of Liberty, *soon announced that the slaves had come through the town on their way to a "southern destination." On 1 September a letter appeared in*

Niles' Weekly Register, *published in Baltimore, in which the unnamed writer claimed to have visited the estate and talked with slaves "whose countenances were remarkably indicative of despondency and dejection. . . . One would have thought that the poor creatures who were left, the aged and blind, had lost every friend on earth." While acknowledging the judge's right to dispose of his chattel, the writer nevertheless contended that "there is something excessively revolting in the fact that a herd of them should be driven from Mount Vernon." Washington learned of all this in early September and quickly accepted an offer from the Federal Republican and Baltimore Telegraph to present his version of events. In describing how fifty-four slaves reacted when sold to Louisiana planters, Washington was either disingenuous or self-deluded.*

BW wrote this letter to Frederick G. Schaeffer on 18 September, and it appeared in the *Union* (Philadelphia), 28 September 1821, which reprinted it from the *Federal Republican and Baltimore Telegraph.*

Sir—I received last night, from Alexandria, your favor of the 11th inst. and I beg you to accept my best thanks for your generous offer of the columns of the Federal Republican for the purpose of refuting certain illiberal remarks, which have appeared in other journals of the day, respecting a sale of negroes which it was my good fortune to effect during the last month.

I had heard that this transaction had been noticed in a Leesburg paper, but in such a manner as to prove that the wound intended to be inflicted was meant, not for me personally, but for the colonization society, through the president of that institution.[1] Niles' Weekly Register of the 1st inst, which was sent to me by a friend on Saturday last, is the only paper which I have seen which contains even an implied censure of my conduct; and had the statement there made corresponded with the truth, it would have passed me unnoticed. It is for the sole purpose of correcting the misrepresentations which appear in that paper that I am induced to avail myself of your offer; but before I do so, I take the liberty, on my own behalf and on that of my southern fellow citizens, to enter a solemn protest against the propriety of any person questioning our right, *legal* or *moral,* to dispose of property which is secured to us by sanctions equally valid with those by which we hold other species of property. . . .

I take no exception, *individually,* to the statement in the Leesburg paper. The simple fact, that a sale was made of 54 negroes, to two gentlemen of Louisiana, is true. . . . I shall pass on to the additional statement to be found in Niles' Register, above alluded to.

How correct it was in the person who made that statement, to visit Mount Vernon in my absence and there to hold conversations with my negroes upon the delicate topics which obviously caused his visit, or was the consequence of it, I submit to his own sense of propriety and to the public judgment to decide. But I surely have a right to complain, that he not only gave credit to himself to the assertions of *such informers,* but that he should publish them to the world, *as facts,* without first applying to me to admit, deny, or explain them. If he had rode one mile, to the house of my nearest neighbor, who is acquainted with every circumstance attending this transaction, he would have received such information as could not, I think, have failed to satisfy him of the falsity of the reports to which he had listened. With those observations upon the conduct of this person, I proceed to notice his statement, the manifest object of which is, not to deny, as it would seem, my *legal* right to dispose of this species of property, although he, as well as the editor of the Register, plainly questions a *moral* right in *me* to ex[er]cise it, but to attach to my conduct the charge of inhumanity in the *mode* of doing it. The charge is

Bushrod Washington, seen here in a nineteenth-century engraving by James B. Longacre, owned the mansion and four thousand acres of Mount Vernon from 1802 until his death in 1829. He also received George Washington's personal and official papers and his library. (Courtesy of the Virginia Historical Society, Richmond)

"that husbands had been torn from their wives and children, and that many relations were left behind."

If the writer of the above letter meant to insinuate that I had *voluntarily* separated husbands from their wives and children, he has been misled by false information. In making out the list of those negroes which, as it will presently appear, I was under the necessity of parting with, I took care so to arrange it, as to avoid the separation of families. There were three or four women in the number, whose husbands were the property of other persons. I immediately opened a negotiation with the owner of two of them, for their purchase, which I should have accomplished, if the husbands had not themselves interposed, and prevented it, by expressing their unwillingness to be sold. Similar overtures were made, as I understand, by those who purchased from me, to the owners of the other husbands, which failed of success from the same cause.

The charge, that parents were torn from their children, if it be meant that I might have prevented such separations, and failed to do so, is equally without foundation. It is well known to those friends to whom a reference will hereafter be made, what sacrifices I submitted to, in order to keep the families entire, and to relieve the members of them from every regret which their change of situation might otherwise have occasioned. I parted with a few negroes, the sons of some of those who were sold, and whose services I know not how to dispense with, at prices greatly below what I would have taken for them from others, and I would cheerfully have given one-third of those prices to retain them, if my feelings could have permitted me to do so. Five young women, the daughters of some that were sold, belonged to other persons, to two of whom offers were made, but without effect, of prices exceeding those which I had obtained. Two out of the five were purchased, and I undertook, without authority, and upon my own responsibility, to sell one of them, the property of a distant nephew, but in whose affection for me, I trusted for an apology.

It is, after all, an extraordinary circumstance, that, whilst emigration to this country of parents who have voluntarily seperated themselves from their children, and of children who have left behind them their parents, never to revisit their native homes, pass daily before our eyes, without observation, so much sensibility should be felt, when similar occurrences take place in relation to this particular class of people.[2] I may be permitted to add, that I have never heard a sigh or a complaint from the parents of the two most valuable servants I ever owned, that their sons had abandoned them and my service, and sought new habitations in the northern states, where they now are.

That the writer of the letter may have observed dejection in the countenances of some of the negroes with whom he conversed at Mount Vernon, on account of a separation from their former companions, is possible, because it was natural. But it is well known to those who were witnesses of the separation, that those who were sold, carried with them no feelings of despondency or regret. In answer to a short address which I made to them, the elders admitted the necessity which compelled me to part with them, and confiding in the assurance made to them by the respectable gentlemen to whom they were sold, as to the treatment they might expect, they expressed their belief that their situation would be improved, and cheerfully consented to go with them. Their behavior during the two days that they remained in Alexandria, indicated a continuance of these feelings, and the almost unlimited licence allowed them by their new masters, proved how confidently they trusted in the sincerity of their declarations.

I pass by the *insinuation*, that, because Gen. Washington thought proper to emancipate his slaves,[3] his nephew ought to do so likewise, with the single observation, that I do not admit the right of any person to decide for me on this point. I am the last man in the world who would attempt to depreciate that, or any other act of this most revered relative.

He was influenced on that, as on all other occasions, by that moral recti-
tude which invariably governed him through life. He believed the measure to be right, and this was always decisive with him. . . .

It is somewhat mortifying to me, th[at] it never occurred to the visitor at Mount Vernon, who seems to have taken so great an interest in my
concerns, to enquire of my manager, or of some one of my neighbors,
what were the motives which had induced me to make this sale? Had he
done so, he would have been informed that the prominent ones were the
following:

1. That I had struggled for about 20 years to pay the expenses of my
farm, and to afford a comfortable support to those who cultivated it,
from the produce of their labour. In this way to have balanced that
account, would have satisfied me. But I always had to draw upon my
other resources for those objects, and I would state upon my best judgment, that the produce of the farm has in general fallen short of its support from $500 to $1000 annually. To the best of my recollection I have
during the above period, (two years excepted,) had to buy corn for the
negroes, for which I have sometimes paid 5, 6, and 7 dollars the barrel.
Last year I commenced the purchase of this article for 90 negroes in the
month of May, and so continued to the end of it.

2d. The insubordination of my negroes, and their total disregard of all
authority, rendered them worse than useless to me. Southern gentlemen
understand, and well know how to appreciate the force of this motive
and I therefore forbear to enlarge upon it.

But if it should be asked, as it well may be, why this temper was more
observable at Mount Vernon, than upon other plantations in the neighborhood, I answer, that, that place has at times been visited by some
unworthy persons, who have condescended to hold conversations with
my negroes, and to impress upon their minds the belief that, as the
nephew of general Washington, or as president of the colonization soci-

ety, or for other reasons, I could not hold them in bondage, and particularly that they would be free *at my death*. That such conversations have passed, I have evidence entirely satisfactory to myself; and that such impressions have been made on the minds of the negroes, was imparted to me by a friend, who had no reason to doubt the fact. In consequence of information so truly alarming, I called the negroes together in March last, and after stating to them what I had heard and that they had been deceived by those who had neither their or my good in view, I assured them most solemnly, that I had no intention to give freedom to any of them, and that nothing but a voluntary act of mine could make them so. That the disappointment caused by this declaration, should lead to the consequences which followed, and which will be mentioned under the next head, was to be expected.

3. The last motive which I deem it necessary to assign was, that I had good reason for anticipating the escape of all the labouring men of any value to the northern states as soon as I should leave home. During my last circuit,[4] and soon after my return, three of them eloped without the pretence of a cause—one of them, a valuable cook, is at this time a fugitive in one of the northern states; the other two were retaken on their way to Pennsylvania—but I had to pay about $250 on these accounts.

I conclude by stating, that the sale of the 54 negroes was made to Mr. Sprigg and Mr. Williams, two gentlemen on the Red River, who meant to place them upon their own estates, and to keep them together. From such purchasers, I was induced to take $2500 less than the price which I had at first fixed upon. . . .

1. BW was the first president of the American Colonization Society, established in 1816 to promote the repatriation of freed blacks to Africa. The society was instrumental in founding Liberia.

2. In this remark BW likened European emigration to the capture and forced removal of Africans from their homeland.

3. In his 1799 will GW manumitted all of the slaves he owned; the Custis dower slaves descended to the heirs of Martha Washington upon her death.

4. That is, BW's circuit as a Supreme Court justice.

1822

PUBLIC PROPERTY?
Charles H. Ruggles

Charles Ruggles's letter to his sister encompasses two themes that recurred repeatedly so long as Washington family members owned Mount Vernon. First, visitors claimed putative possession, despite the estate's status as private property and a working plantation. Second, the word "decay" appeared in narratives; opinions varied as to what that meant and who was responsible.

This letter, dated 28 April, to Sarah C. Ruggles is among the holdings of the Mount Vernon Ladies' Association and is used with permission.

. . . I have just returned from Mount Vernon a place to which few of the visitors of Washington [D.C.] neglect to go, and a place which I would not willingly have gone home without seeing. Mr Sibley of Michigan and Mr Schoolcraft the author & numerologist were of the party. It is 14 miles from this city; and in a hack and 4 horses we went rapidly.

Judge Washington and his family are at Philadelphia, and the custom seems to be both in his absence and when he is at home to go over his grounds and through his house with very little ceremony. The fame of General Washington is the property of the nation, and individuals appear to consider the mansion and lands which formerly belonged to him, so far public property as to entitle them to run through them and round them without regard to the convenience of the present proprietor.

Indeed it seems to be reasonable that the successor to the estate of so illustrious a man should permit any of his Countrymen to examine whatever may awaken recollections of his greatness or afford a glimpse of his private life.

Mount Vernon is by nature a most beautiful place. The house is of wood—old, plain, and has rather a gothic appearance. It was built by Laurence Washington. The General added to it a piazza of more modern fashion than the original building, and two wings which have nothing to distinguish them from farmhouse architecture. A stranger is struck with the plainness, and I may add, the stiffness of appearance by which the whole is characterized. It would perhaps be unfair to judge of General Washingtons taste by what we now see, because he did not originally build the house; and because its appearance may be changed since his death. The changes which have taken place are, however, chiefly produced by decay—few from purposed alterations: and on the whole one would be led to think that the General paid no great regard to ornament and that in whatever he attempted in that way he was unsuccessful. The green house now contains a great number of coffee trees, pine apples, and plaintains besides oranges, lemons and exotic flowers. Many of the ornamental trees and shrubs appear to have been planted promiscuously, without order or regularity. This was far more agreeable to my eye than the sharp points and angles in which the box[wood] borders of the garden were arranged.

The key of the French Bastile hangs in a glass box in the Hall. It was sent to Gen. W. by the Marquis de LaFayete. A huge, rusty, old fashioned thing it is.

The tomb which contains his ashes is but a short distance from the house. I plucked a branch of the cedar which grows upon it a part of which I send you. There is no stone or inscription to denote to a stranger where his remains are deposited.

117

1822

No Eating, Drinking, and Dancing Parties Allowed
Bushrod Washington

In more ways than one, Bushrod Washington had an uneasy relationship with members of the public who visited the estate. He was particularly displeased at the behavior of some who arrived on steamboats that cruised the Potomac River, beginning at Washington, D.C., and Alexandria. When, despite his protestations, steamboats continued to land passengers at Mount Vernon, the judge published this handbill detailing the sources of his displeasure. In an addendum he threatened legal action against offending boat captains.

This handbill of 4 July is among the holdings of the Mount Vernon Ladies' Association and is used with permission.

NOTICE.

THE feelings of Mrs. Washington and myself, have been so much wounded by some late occurrences at this place, that I am compelled to give this PUBLIC NOTICE, that permission will not in future, be granted to Steam-Boat Parties, to enter the Gardens, or to walk over the grounds, nor will I consent that Mount Vernon, much less the Lawn, shall be the place at which eating, drinking and dancing parties may assemble.

It is not my wish by a particular recital of the unpleasant circumstances, which have led to this notice, to give offence to any person; but I may be permitted to state generally, as my opinion, that a stranger who had accidentally stopped here upon many of the occasions alluded to, not knowing to whom the place had belonged, would hardly have taken it for the residence of a private gentleman.

The respect which I owe to the memory of my revered *uncle*, and that which I claim for myself, forbid my longer submitting to similar indignities. Respectable strangers and others, be their condition in life what it may, who may be led by curiosity to visit this place, will at all times, (Sundays always excepted) receive the same attention which has heretofore been uniformly and cheerfully shown such characters.

1823

THE FOURTH OF JULY
From the *National Intelligencer*

Elaborate ceremonial events occasionally were staged at the estate, including one on the Fourth of July in 1823, in which Bushrod Washington and his wife, Julia Ann Blackburn Washington, participated. The presence of elderly soldiers of the Revolution added special poignancy and meaning to the day.

This account is in "Celebrations of the 4th of July at Mount Vernon," *National Intelligencer* (Washington, D.C.), 9 July 1823.

Having been politely permitted by Judge Washington to celebrate the 47th Anniversary of American Independence, at the tomb of the Father of his country—a numerous and respectable party of citizens of this place,[1] with several strangers of distinction, assembled at an early hour, agreeably to previous arrangement, on board the steamboat *Washington*, and proceeded to Alexandria, where they were joined by a party from that city.

The day was propitious, and the passage to Mount Vernon uncommonly delightful, which was heightened by the appropriate music of a full band from the marine corps, furnished by the politeness of Col. Henderson.

There was no heart that did not harmonise with the occasion, and throb with emotion, in contemplating the repository of his remains who had achieved the liberties they were about to commemorate. The landscape around, the day, the occasion, all conspired to produce feelings at once elevating and grateful.

When the boat arrived in sight of that sacred spot, the band struck up the plaintive air of Roslin Castle.[2]

The committee of arrangements debarked and proceeded to pay their respects to the proprietor of the ground, to notify him of the arrival of the company, and to select a suitable place for the performance of the appointed exercises.

The committee then returned; when the company landed, and formed, under the direction of Col. Brearly, chief marshal, in the following order of procession:

1. The band of music.

2. The clergy, supported on the right and left by the committee of arrangements.

3. The orator of the day, and reader, supported in the same manner.

4. Revolutionary officers.

5. Officers of the Army and Navy.

6. French Legation.

7. Distinguished strangers.

8. Citizens.

The procession proceeded to the pavilion[3] near the sepulchre of Washington, where a party of ladies had already assembled to participate in the services of the day.

The Rev. Mr. Ryland opened with an impressive prayer.

George H. Richards, Esq. followed in an oration peculiarly adapted to the occasion, and full of eloquence.

Julia Ann Blackburn Washington, the wife of Bushrod Washington.
Undated portrait attributed to Chester Harding. (Collection of the Supreme Court
of the United States; photograph by Vic Boswell. Used with permission)

C. W. Goldsborough, Esq. after a pertinent introduction, read Washington's Farewell Address; and the whole was concluded with a fervent prayer by the Rev. Mr. Post, for a blessing on the services, and the universal diffusion of liberty.

After these services, and during the interchange of friendly salutations between Judge Washington and the individuals composing the company, in which he expressed his thanks for the tribute of respect paid to the memory of his revered uncle, the band were saluting Mrs. Washington in the piazza of the mansion.

The procession formed again; and, opening to the right and left, encircled the tomb. A solemn silence now pervaded the company, which was broken only by the beat of the muffled drum at the door of the vault, and the sympathizing music of Pleyel's Hymn poured out by the full band.

Considering the time and place, the effect of this scene, in the midst of the sacred grove, was singularly awful and sublime.

After the music ceased there was an involuntary lingering round the spot; and the hearts of all were melted, when, looking up, they saw a venerable survivor of Rochambeau's army mingling his tears with those of American patriotism.

The procession descended to the shore, and reimbarked, much gratified and deeply impressed with the exercises and the scene they had witnessed.

The company, on their return to Alexandria, sat down to an elegant dinner.

1. Washington, D.C.

2. A Scottish air frequently used in the Continental army for burial services.

3. This is a reference to a structure commonly called the summer house, built during BW's tenure. See the illustration on p. 14.

1824
LAFAYETTE'S RETURN
Auguste Levasseur

At the invitation of the federal government, Lafayette, hero of the Amer-
ican Revolution and passionate advocate of human liberty, returned to
the United States in 1824 after an absence of forty years. In an extraordi-
nary tour during which he traveled to every state in the Union, he was
fêted with lavish parades and ceremonies in which millions of Americans
participated. Alongside the grand theme of Lafayette's tour—namely,
the success of the American experiment in building a self-governing
republic—stood another: the passing of the Revolutionary generation.
Lafayette fondly, sometimes tearfully, embraced aged veterans and
met with widows of men long dead. When he revisited Mount Vernon
in October 1824, the experience proved overwhelming, as his personal
secretary recounts here. Lafayette sanctified Mount Vernon as no other
living person could have done, for besides being the last surviving general
officer of the Continental army, he had enjoyed a paternally close rela-
tionship with Washington.

This depiction is in *Lafayette, Guest of the Nation: A Contemporary Account*
of the "Triumphal Tour" of General Lafayette through the United States in
1824–1825 as Reported by the Local Newspapers, compiled and edited by Edgar
E. Brandon, 3 vols. (Oxford, Oh., 1950–57), 3:42–43.

On the 17th, we embarked on board of the steamboat *Petersburg,* having
on board the Minister of War, Mr. Calhoun,[1] Generals M'Comb and
Jones, and a great number of other officers, as well as many citizens.
After two hours sailing, the cannon of Fort Washington, announced to
us that we were approaching the last asylum of the elder son of American

liberty. At this mournful signal, to which the band that accompanied us, replied in plaintive tones, we mounted to the deck, and the lands of Mount Vernon presented themselves to our view. At that sight, an involuntary and spontaneous movement, inclined us to bend our knees. Our landing was facilitated by boats; and we soon trod the soil which had so often been trod by Washington. A coach received General Lafayette and the other travellers, which silently ascended the steep path that led to the solitary habitation of Mount Vernon. On recrossing that hospitable threshold, which had offered him a refuge, when the crimes of others had violently torn him from his country and his family, George Washington Lafayette[2] felt his heart affected, in no longer finding there, him whose paternal care had comforted him in misfortune—him whose examples and wise instructions, had inspired his youthful mind with those generous sentiments, which at the present day, render him an example to good citizens—a model for fathers and husbands, a most devoted son, and most faithful friend; and his father[3] looked about with tenderness for everything that might recal the companion of his glorious labours.

Three nephews of Washington came to receive the General, his son, and myself, to conduct us to the tomb of their uncle.[4] Our numerous travelling companions entered the house, and a few moments afterwards, the cannon of the fort, thundering anew, announced to the surrounding country that Lafayette was paying respect to the ashes of Washington. Simple and modest as he was during his life, so he appears in his last repose. The tomb of the citizen-hero is hardly perceptible through the black cypresses which surround it. A little rising ground covered with turf, a wooden door without an inscription, a few faded garlands, and others still green, show to the traveller who visits this place, the spot where he reposes in peace, whose powerful arm broke the chains of his country.

On our approach the door was opened. General Lafayette first descended into the tomb, and a few moments afterwards returned to the threshold, his face wet with tears. He took his son and myself by the hand, and made us enter with him, and showed us by a sign the coffin of his paternal friend. He reposes by the side of her who was his companion during life, and whom death has now united with him forever. We prostrated ourselves together before that coffin, which we respectfully touched with our lips. On rising, we threw ourselves into the arms of General Lafayette, and mingled our tears and our regrets with his.

On leaving the tomb, we found the three nephews of Washington ardently praying for their uncle, and mingling in their prayers the name of Lafayette. One of them, Mr. Custis,[5] offered the General a gold ring, containing some of the hair of the great man; and we returned by the path to the house, where our travelling companions were awaiting us. An hour was devoted to visiting the house and gardens, which are now the property of a nephew of Washington, bearing his name; and occupying one of the first offices in the American magistracy.[6] He was determined to make no change in the estate left him by his uncle, to whose memory he pays the most respectful and most tender regard. Mr. George W. Lafayette assured me that every thing in the house was still much in the same state in which he had left it twenty-eight years ago. He found in the place where Washington had put it, the principal key of the Bastille, which Lafayette sent him after the destruction of that monument of despotism. The note which accompanied it is still carefully preserved along with the key.

After a few moments of repose we again took the path which leads down to the shore. Our march was a silent one. Each of us bore in his hand a branch of cypress, cut from over the tomb of Washington. We might have seemed an afflicted family, returning from committing to the earth a father dearly beloved, who had been removed by death. We were already on board, and had proceeded far over the rapid waves, before any person broke the silence of meditation. At length Mount Vernon disappeared behind the winding and elevated banks of the river, when all assembled in the stern of the vessel, and listened attentively until evening, while General Lafayette spoke of Washington.

1. John C. Calhoun.

2. General Lafayette's son, who, to escape the ravages of the French Revolution, arrived in the United States and lived with the Washingtons in the 1790s. See the account of Benjamin Henry Latrobe, 1796, above.

3. General Lafayette.

4. Lewis Washington is the only nephew identified by name in Levasseur's account.

5. George Washington Parke Custis.

6. BW was not at home during Lafayette's visit.

1826

SHOCK AND CONSOLATION
Thomas Hayes

Coming upon the old tomb, Thomas Hayes at first was shocked at its forlorn appearance and the absence of any monument. Then he reconsidered.

This letter, dated 26 April, appears among the holdings of the Mount Vernon Ladies' Association and is used with permission.

Yesterday paid a visit to Mount Vernon and saw the Tomb in which are deposited the mortal remains of the Imortal Washington. I can scarsely my dear Parents convey to you an Idea of my feelings on my approach to the Spot. Nothing but a few coarse bricks and a mound of earth to mark the grave of the Father of his Country. Good God thought I to myself is it possible that the American Nation can have pass'd over this so negligently[?] Had he have liv'd in pass't ages all the wealth of the Nation would not have been considered to[o] much to have rais'd a Monument to his Memory, but upon reflection we find that he has a Monument more precious, more valuable than all the marble that could be erected. It is that that is inherent in the heart of evry American, and in the honest and true praise of a gratefull nation.

1826

IMPROPRIETIES AND THREATS
From the *Microcosm*

When Bushrod Washington refused to admit a party of United States congressmen to the grounds one May morning, the encounter received widespread publicity. Included in this newspaper article is the suggestion that, owing to the judge's lack of cooperation, the remains of George Washington should be removed to a place where public accessibility could be guaranteed. Following the article is a rejoinder in defense of the judge.

This article appeared in the *National Journal* (Washington, D.C.) and, subsequently, in numerous newspapers, including the *Microcosm* (Providence, R.I.), 26 May 1826, from which it and the rejoinder are reprinted here.

It is rumoured that a party consisting of about thirty members of Congress, of both Houses, wishing to visit the tomb of Washington, hired the steam-boat "Enterprise," and proceeded in her to Mount Vernon, on the 14th inst. After the boat had gone some distance, and before they reached Mount Vernon, it was stated to them by the Captain, that Judge Washington, the proprietor of the place, had forbid persons from landing from on board of a steam-boat, at Mount Vernon. The gentlemen thinking that a refusal could not be given, appointed a Committee consisting of three of their body, to wait upon Judge Washington, and to ask the permission of him of paying their respects to the seat of the deceased Father of their Independence. This was done in the most polite and respectful manner by the Committee, who went on shore for the purpose, the other gentlemen remaining on board the steam-boat. The permission was refused, and it is said, the Committee was not treated with common politeness, and the refusal was accompanied by threats of instituting suits, &c. Is it possible that this report is true? If so, ought it not to be a good reason why Congress ought to remove the remains of Washington from a place to which his grateful country-men cannot go to perform that pilgrimage which will be made, as long as gratitude is a virtue or love of country warms the bosom of an American. For the honour of the name of "Washington," we can scarcely believe the report, and it comes from such authority we cannot doubt it.

A Rejoinder
From the *Phoenix Gazette*

The cause of these gentlemen being disappointed in their visit was that they had selected Sunday, as the day for making it. Judge Washington had given public notice, that on Sundays he must decline to admit any one to Mount Vernon, and had informed the captains of steam-boats in particular, that he would be obliged on that day to refuse admission to all persons. After such a notification there was such an obvious impropriety in the course adopted by the members of Congress, who are certainly not exempt from the obligations of society and good breeding, that any censure in the case must attach rather to them than to the occupant of Mount Vernon.

1826

"THESE GROUNDS SHOULD BE THE PROPERTY OF THE NATION"
A Veteran Officer

Whereas Bushrod Washington disparaged the behavior of unannounced congressmen and intrusive strangers, he obviously welcomed ceremonial visits such as the one described in this anonymously published account. For the young military cadets who were admitted to the tomb and saw "all the curiosities of the estate," the experience was designed to instill veneration for General Washington and attachment to the nation. For the account's author, the event served as a backdrop for a plea that Mount Vernon be made federal property, accessible to the citizenry and perhaps also used as a summer retreat for American presidents.

This account appeared in "Journal of a Veteran Officer," *New-York Mirror. A Weekly Journal, Devoted to Literature and the Fine Arts* (New York City), 28 February 1835.

On the twenty-third day of December, 1826, I joined a party going to visit the tomb of Washington, at Mount Vernon. Captain Partridge, who was a superintendent of a military and scientifick establishment, had marched from the eastern states with a corps of cadets, to visit Washington city and Mount Vernon. He had invited a large proportion of the military officers of the city to join him in the pilgrimage, and they generally attended. I happened to be one of the invited guests. The day was remarkably fine, and our passage down the Potomac in a steamboat pleasant. The year was closing, and the quantity of canvass-back ducks was almost incredible; such numbers I never saw before. On reaching Mount Vernon, Judge Washington received us with the greatest kindness. He sent refreshments to the cadets, and invited the officers and gentlemen who were present to his hospitable mansion. He opened the tomb of his illustrious uncle, and that of many generations of kindred. The coffin of the patriot had been covered with black broadcloth, which was now hanging in strings, and with a holy theft we tore shreds of it to bear away as relicks. Over the tomb, which was a simple excavation in the side of a hill, were growing several handsome trees, mostly oaks, on which hung large bunches of mistletoe in the most perfect green. The cadets, wild and frolicksome as boys of that age are, were penetrated with the solemnity of the scene, and listened to two addresses from the mound which covered the ashes of George Washington. Senator Smith, from Maryland, made a harangue to the youths, and Captain Partridge followed him. The speeches were very good; but no holy emanation came from the shrine below to give a tongue of fire to the orators. They spoke as sensible men; but seemed to draw no inspiration from the place. The politicks of the senator, and the discipline and philosophical precision of the military and scientifick teacher, seemed to destroy all the classical enthusiasm of the speakers. The boys listened, and were improved by the discourses; but no infant hero was born from the glory of the incident. . . .

Judge Washington showed us all the curiosities of the estate. The conservatory and the green-house are in good repair, exhibiting shrubs, plants, and flowers that were given to General Washington by distinguished persons in Europe and in this country. There are hundreds of farms or plantations of more beauty and profit than Mount Vernon. Since the west and south have taken to raising tobacco the land is not profitable, and the slaves on it are a burden to the owner. This gift of Mount Vernon, from Washington to his nephew, was of no value; for probably, from the hour of his death to the present time, the plantation has not supported itself. These grounds should be the property of the nation, never to be sold, but kept as a summer residence of the president of the United States; of course a place where all could visit without trespassing upon private property, which is now done to the annoyance of its owners. The visiters plunder it of branches and shrubs. The domains should be their own. The masonick family once intended to build a monument to the great man at Mount Vernon; but this has not been done. The true affection of a few individuals is often more efficacious in rearing memorials to departed greatness, than the gratitude of nations. . . .

This is a reflection on the many, while they suffer a few to anticipate national feeling, and cover themselves with glory in doing what should be done by all and by common consent. The nation should not suffer this neglect to the memory of the mighty dead to remain any longer. It is a blot on our escutcheon. But it is in vain to attempt to arouse a country; the feelings of a people go by a sort of earthquake shock. There is no calculation about it.

1832

OVERWHELMED BY THE NATION'S HISTORY
From the *Family Magazine*

In 1829 John Augustine Washington inherited the mansion and 1,225 surrounding acres. Through birth and marriage, he and his wife, Jane Charlotte Blackburn Washington, were niece and nephew to Bushrod and Julia Ann Blackburn Washington. The new owner and his family divided their time between Mount Vernon and their home, Blakeley, in Jefferson County, Virginia, where many Washington kin lived on lands originally surveyed and patented by their illustrious kinsman.

The following essay describes a trip to Mount Vernon in the early 1830s. Note that an African American conducted the anonymous author and his or her companions through several rooms of the mansion. Surrounded there and on the grounds by "hallowed associations," the author felt an overwhelming connection to the nation's history. In the words of a later visitor, the site "does this" because "so much of thrilling interest in American history was connected with" Mount Vernon.

This essay was published in "Mount Vernon," *Family Magazine* 4 (1836): 282–84. The material quoted above appeared in E. Kennedy, "Mount Vernon— A Pilgrimage," *Southern Literary Messenger* 18 (1852): 54–55.

We thought to gallop to Mount Vernon (from Alexandria), but the chance of missing the way, and the tiresomeness of a gig, induced us to take a hackney coach. Accordingly, we took magnificent possession, and ordered it on with all convenient despatch. But haste was out of the question—for never was worse road extant than that to Mount Vernon. Still in the season of foliage, it may be a romantick route. As it was, we saw nothing to attract the eye as particularly engaging, save a few seats scattered among the hills, and occupying some picturesque eminences. On we went—and yet onward—through all variety of scenery, hill and vale, meadow and woodland, until a sheet of water began to glimmer through the dim trees, and announce our approach again to the Potomack. In a few moments, a turn in the wild and uneven road brought us in view of the old mansion-house of Washington. We drove to the entrance of the old gate-way, and alighted in the midst of what appeared to be a little village—so numerous and scattered were the buildings. They were of brick, and devoted to the lower menial purposes of the place. As we advanced, the houses that covered the grounds, had a neater appearance, and when we came in view of the edifice of which all these were the outworks or appendages, we were at once struck with the simple beauty of the structure, and the quiet and secluded loveliness of its situation. . . .

Sending in our cards by an old servant, we were soon invited to enter. Not having letters to Mr. W., the present proprietor, who is now very ill, we did not expect to see any of the family. A servant accordingly, at our

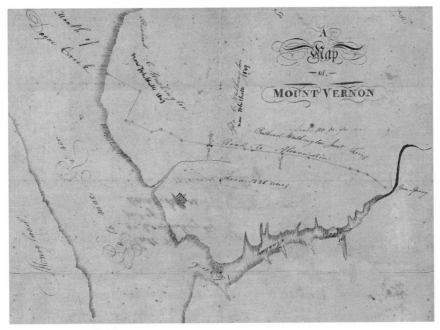

"A Map of Mount Vernon," 1831, shows the land that descended from Bushrod
Washington to his nephew John Augustine Washington in 1829. Before the 1850s
most travelers arrived at the estate via the road from Alexandria.
(Courtesy of the Mount Vernon Ladies' Association)

request, merely accompanied us through the rooms made interesting by
the hallowed associations that came fast upon us as we traversed them.
In the hall or entry, hangs, in a glass case, the key of the [B]astile, which
every body has heard of. It was presented to Washington by La Fayette.
Under it is a picture of that renowned fortress. The key is by no means
formidable for its size; it is about as large as a bank-key, and of a shape
by no means mysterious enough for a dissertation. The only curious portion of it is that grasped by the hand in turning. It is solid and of an oval
shape, and appeared to me, for I always love to be curious in these matters, to have been broken, on a time, and then soldered or brazen again.

133

It probably had some hard wrenches in its day. On the whole, it appeared to be a very amiable key, and by no means equal to all the turns it must have seen in the [French] Revolution.

We were first shown into a small room, which was set apart as the study of Washington. Here he was wont to transact all his business of state, in his retirement. It was hung with pictures and engravings of revolutionary events, and among the miniatures was one of himself, said to be the best likeness ever taken. Another room was shown us which had nothing remarkable about it, and then we passed into a larger one, finished with great taste, and containing a portrait of Judge Washington. A beautiful organ stood in the corner, and the fireplace was adorned by a mantelpiece of most splendid workmanship in bas-relief. It is of Italian marble, and was presented to Washington by La Fayette.[1] This part of our visit was soon over. There was little to see in the house, and the portions referred to were all to which we were admitted. I could not help admiring, however, the neatness and air of antiquity together, which distinguished the several rooms through which we passed. There was something, also, fanciful in their arrangement, that was quite pleasing to my eye, far more so, than the mathematical exactness and right-angleism of modern and more splendid mansions. I like these old houses and quaint apartments that tell you fantastick tales of their first proprietors, and of their architects; and, as you wander through them, something of the olden time comes upon you, that you would not away with, if you could— or could not, if you would.

Passing from the house, down a rude pathway, and then over a little broken but already verdant ground, we came to an open space, and found ourselves standing before the humble tomb of George Washington. It was a happy moment to visit the spot. There was something in the time, fortunate for the feelings. The very elements seemed in accordance with the season. The day was beautiful—the sunlight was streaming full upon the trees round about and glowing with a mellow beam upon the grave; the place was quiet, and the only sound that we heard save that of our own hearts, was the voice of the wind through the pines, or of the waters as they broke upon the shore below us. Who can analyze his feelings as he stands before that sepulchre? Who can tell the story of his associations, or do justice by his tongue or his pen to the emotions which the memories of the past awaken there! The history of a whole country is overpowering him at once. Its struggle—its darkness—its despair—its victory rush upon him. Its gratitude, its glory, and its loss, pass before him—and in a few moments he lives through an age of interest and wonder. Strange power of the human mind! What an intimation does this rapid communion with the past, and with the spirits of the past, give, at once, of their immortality and our own! But it is [in] vain to follow out these feelings here. They would fill volumes.

There is no inscription on the tomb. . . . There is a total absence of every thing like parade or circumstance about the resting-place of the Hero and Father. He sleeps there in the midst of the simplicities of nature. Cypress-trees wave over his dust on every side, and the traveller, who goes to stand by his grave finds no careful enclosure to forbid his too near approach.

1. The gift came from Samuel Vaughan, not Lafayette.

1832

A Death in the Family
The Account of an Anonymous Physician

John Augustine and Jane Charlotte Washington struggled to maintain domestic privacy in a place inundated with strangers whose behavior ranged from reverential to intrusive. As John's health deteriorated in 1831

The master bed chamber, painted by John Gadsby Chapman, ca. 1833.
(Courtesy of the Homeland Foundation, Inc., Amenia, N.Y.)

and 1832, probably owing to tuberculosis, the presence of visitors caused added strain. The climax came in June 1832, here recorded by an unidentified physician.

This depiction is in "Skeleton of Manuscript," by George Washington Ball, n.d., among the Ball Family Papers, 1716–1983, held by the Virginia Historical Society, Richmond, and is used with permission.

He had been ill a long time: had frequent attacks of hemorrhage from the lungs; in one of which, though not at that time residing near enough to be his regular physician, I happened to be attending him.

Mrs. Washington and myself were sitting by his bedside, one morning, keeping him very quiet, when, suddenly, we heard a commotion in the lower part of the house.

Jane C. Washington holds the family Bible in this painting by John
Gadsby Chapman, ca. 1833. Next to her are daughter Anna Maria and son
Richard Blackburn Washington. The eldest son, John Augustine Washington,
stands at the right. The boy in front of her is a nephew, Noblet Herbert, whom
Jane raised after his parents died. (Courtesy of the George Washington
Masonic National Memorial Association, Alexandria, Va.)

The patient excitedly demanding to know what was the matter, I went out to investigate, and found, below, a party of strangers, who, in spite of the protestations of the servants that their master lay ill, had forced an entrance into the Hall, and were insisting on going through a portion of the rooms.

Before the clamor could be stilled, I was recalled by a piercing shriek from Mrs Washington, hastened back, and found her husband lying forward upon the bed, with the blood pouring from his mouth. In a very few minutes he was a corpse!

Ten minutes later, I again went down, and found the party still lingering on the portico. When informed of what they had done they looked as though they wished the earth to open and swallow them up, hurried to their carriages and drove off.

1833

"A GLORIOUS REMEMBRANCE"
Caroline Moore

John Augustine Washington bequeathed his property to his wife, who, with their young children, continued the practice of dividing their time between Mount Vernon and Blakeley. At Jane Charlotte Washington's direction, unexpected visitors were not admitted to the mansion, but she willingly allowed them to stroll the grounds under the guidance of African Americans attached to the estate. Some were slaves who had belonged to Bushrod Washington; others Jane owned; and into the 1830s a few African Americans manumitted by George Washington continued to live there as well. Caroline Moore's journal reflects the growing role that African Americans played in greeting travelers, conducting them to points of interest, and reminiscing about Washington and eighteenth-

century Mount Vernon. Following one such experience Caroline Moore, a Bostonian, expressed the intense emotional hold that the site continued to exert.

This journal excerpt is among the holdings of the Mount Vernon Ladies' Association and is used with permission.

Tuesday April 30th 1833.

A bright spot on the page of my exertion. At 9 AM we left Washington in a carriage for Mount Vernon!!!

. . . On arriving at the porters' lodge the gate was opened by an old black woman, and we were ushered into the Manor of Mount Vernon. I cannot describe my feelings when we first entered the domains. . . .

We rode ½ a mile to the Mansion over as bad a road as can be imagined. The Avenue is shockingly neglected.

On our arrival at the gate of the mansion an aged negro came to us, and offered to escort us over the grounds, observing that no strangers were permitted to enter the house as Mrs Washington (the relict of Mr John Washington recently dead) was residing there with her children. We regretted this arrangement very much as we were very desirous of visiting the library and seeing the Key of the Bastile in the entry, but notwithstanding our earnest desire[,] the extreme heat of the day, and Mr Vase sending in our cards, no notice was taken of our request.

Our guide first took us to the tomb where the remains of General Washington are now interred. They were removed from the old tomb about 3 years since. . . . Near his Tomb, you see the burying place of his slaves, containing 150 graves. We then walked to the Old tomb, which is situated on the Bank of the Potomac; it is in a very ruinous condition.

We went into a dilapidated summer house near it, to rest ourselves, and get a little cool as the heat was excessive. It was an interesting spot

John Gadsby Chapman's engraving of the new Washington family tomb was published in the *Family Magazine* (1835–36). This is the only known image of the tomb as originally constructed, without the elaborate antechamber and iron gate added later. (Courtesy of the Wisconsin Historical Society, Madison. Image ID: 28319)

to sit in. On one side washed the waters of the Potomac, as smooth as a summer sea, and on the other the mansion and grounds of Washington, and the delightful and hallowed conviction that we were really at Mount Vernon. We walked some distance on the Bank of the river, passed the house, went to the door of one of the negro houses and requested a glass of water which was readily handed to us, therefore we had the satisfaction of drinking water at Mount Vernon.

The name of our guide was Oliver Smith, aged about seventy years.[1] He was *raised* he said by the father of the late Judge Washington and

"Summer-House at Mount Vernon," sketched by Benson J. Lossing and reproduced in his *Mount Vernon and Its Associations: Historical, Biographical, and Pictorial* (1859). (Courtesy of Special Collections, University of Virginia Library)

became the property of his son. He was often in the habit of accompanying his master to Mount Vernon in the days of the General, and the old man appeared to feel deeply the neglect which characterised the place, and wished we could have seen the mansion and ground as they were when the General was alive. We visited the Green House and Garden both of which appeared in better order than any thing else we saw. I never saw so large lemon & orange trees, we saw a Sago tree, which was planted by the General's own hand as the Gardener said, who was the son of Oliver.[2]

My reflections while standing by the tomb of Washington were as follows, hurried and crude enough. Oliver was plucking some of the cypress for us.

I stood like one dreaming and somewhat doubting my identity, my feelings were various. I felt grateful for the privilege of visiting this consecrated spot, and thought I could not fully enjoy the present, but what a glorious reminiscence it would be when at home, when the excitement had passed and left the deep, calm impression upon my memory. While there, the dreary desolation of the scene, cast a shade of melancholy over my thoughts.

Every thing around bore evident marks of neglect and decay, and seemed to utter a language more forcibly than words to the interested beholder. *The Master spirit is gone.* The energy and industry which caused every thing in that delightful spot to flourish, has ceased and the taste and judgement which dictated the improvements are no more.

The time spent at Mount Vernon was a season of deep reflection, and will never be effaced from my mind.

Not a human being or an animal now exists there, who were wont to minister to the comfort or pleasure of the great and good man, and every thing around gave a forcible intimation of the vanity of worldly desires. Nothing was left of Washington—but his imperishable name, and the glorious example he has left to posterity.

After passing two hours in a state of intense interest we left Mount Vernon, and rode to Alexandria, where we arrived at 4 P.M. fatigued, hungry & thirsty, and we found that the feelings of the morning, had not entirely destroyed our wish for a good dinner, which was immediately placed upon the table, and we did ample justice to it.

1. A list of slaves that Bushrod Washington compiled in 1815 included fifty-five-year-old Oliver, who originally belonged to BW's father, John Augustine Washington (d. 1787).

2. Other accounts identify the gardener as Phil, who, according to BW's slave list, was twenty-five years old in 1815.

1834
Going to Ruin
Benjamin Brown French

With increasing frequency in the 1830s, observers commented on the estate's seeming decline. Among them was Benjamin Brown French, who visited Mount Vernon several times during the years he served as clerk of the United States House of Representatives.

This account is in *Witness to the Young Republic: A Yankee's Journal, 1828–1870*, edited by Donald B. Cole and John J. McDonough, 42–43, © 1989 by the University Press of New England, Hanover, N.H., and is reprinted with permission.

Friday, May 23. This day Mrs. French & myself have been to Mount Vernon. . . .

Everything except the garden & interior of the house appears to be going to ruin. The old tomb is fast crumbling away, & over the door is an aperture through which I looked. It contains old boxes (probably the outside coffins, in which the remains of those who have heretofore been placed in the tomb were enclosed) broken to pieces, & thrown in a pile at the farther part. The new tomb is built in a spot selected by Washington himself, and of brick burned by him for the purpose previous to his decease. It is roughly built, the front shewing rough brickwork, in the centre of which is a small iron door, hung in a stone doorcase. Directly over this door is a stone tablet on which is that part of the burial service commencing "I am the resurrection and the life," etc. At the

143

top, above the tablet, is inscribed on stone, "The Washington Family." The tomb is built upon inclining ground. It is covered with earth, & there is a quantity of *old brush* thrown onto it, through which all manner of weeds are making their way. From it I plucked a sprig of evergreen & a weed. The garden, containing several acres, is kept in excellent order, & is filled with greenhouse plants, Lemons, oranges, etc., & the walks are beautifully arranged & bordered with box[wood]. The greenhouse was empty, the plants having been yesterday all taken out & placed about the garden. An old servant, who went about with us, called the garden "the West Indies." He pointed out to us the windows of the chamber in which Washington died. He was not one of the General's slaves, but a slave of his brother who resided in Alexandria, & he used to be at Mount Vernon almost daily & was well acquainted with the General.[1]

Our visit was very pleasant, and as I passed about the grounds & stood before the tomb, I thought how many illustrious individuals had passed in the very footpaths I was traversing & had stood where I then was, & paid to the shade of the mighty man whose remains were there deposited the tribute of gratitude for a Free & Independent Country. I thought of the good Lafayette, of Jefferson, Madison & Monroe, & I doubted whether ever another man would live, in America, whose memory would be so dearly cherished as that of George Washington.

1. The slave apparently claimed as his master John Augustine Washington (d. 1787), the favorite brother of GW and the father of Bushrod Washington. The assertion of nearly daily visits to Mount Vernon is almost certainly apocryphal.

The old tomb, although no longer in use after the mid-1830s, continued to attract visitors. This painting by Russell Smith, ca. 1839, reveals its dilapidated condition and suggests the ineffectiveness, by then, of fences erected to keep people from walking on top of the vault. (Courtesy of the Mount Vernon Ladies' Association)

1834
MECCA OF THE MIND
From the *New-England Magazine*

This anonymously published account presents a typical encounter with the estate during the 1830s. Like her uncle Bushrod, Jane Charlotte Washington forbade steamboat passengers from entering the grounds, which, considering the notoriously poor road from Alexandria, almost certainly diminished the number of pilgrims willing to make the trip. Once at Mount Vernon, travelers became fascinated with slaves thought to have known the living Washington—to the extent that fact and fiction mingled. Thus, assuming that the writer of this account accurately repeated a conversation with Oliver Smith, the old slave gardener claimed George Washington as master, when in fact he had belonged to Washington's brother John and subsequently descended to Bushrod, John Augustine, and Jane C. Washington. In naming the general as his master, Oliver Smith pleased visitors by lending immediacy and authenticity to tales already familiar to many of them. People in the 1830s also saw and described the incomplete new tomb, built on the site Washington had chosen. Finally, as extensive carving of names and initials on the summer house attests, people longed to leave behind some token of their presence, even as they carried away souvenir twigs, stones, and other "relics."

This observer's portrayal appeared in "An Hour at Mount Vernon," *New-England Magazine* 7 (1834): 398–400.

> Such graves as his are pilgrim-shrines,
> Shrines to no code or creed confined,—
> The Delphian vales, the Palestines,
> The Meccas of the mind. HALLECK

A visit to Mount Vernon is among the first attractions, which present themselves to the *ennuyé* in Washington. Formerly the steam-boats, which ply up and down the river, could transport you to this spot; but now, passengers, who adopt this mode of conveyance, are prohibited from landing; and, if you would see the last resting-place of the Father of his Country, you must consent to be jolted ten or twenty miles over the most execrable road that necks were ever broken upon. . . .

One delicious morning, [in] May, in company with a friend, I took the steam-boat for Alexandria, with the view of finding some conveyance thence to Mount Vernon. The brimmed Potomac was flashing and streaming, like molten silver, in the sunshine. We skimmed along its smooth surface at a tolerable speed, although our boat was small, incommodious, and very loose in its joints. Every motion of the machinery seemed as if it would shake it in pieces. There was a miscellaneous assemblage of passengers on board. . . .

Alexandria is little more than eight miles from the capitol, and, as we approached the city, it appeared to great advantage. We here succeeded in obtaining a horse and gig, and, thus provided, we set out upon our pilgrimage. I will not indulge myself in any anathemas upon the roads. As the last new novel happily observes, "they may be more easily conceived than described." In many places we found logs and branches embedded in the loamy soil, or filling up the numerous excavations, caused by the rains. Occasionally half a dozen protruding stumps would bristle before us, so ingeniously arranged, as to render it a seeming impossibility to prevent our wheels from striking against every one of them. Now and then an abrupt slope would invite our poor beast to upset us; but fortunately he was too conscientious an animal to attempt it. He carried us patiently along, at an even pace, and, at last, after passing through a considerable extent of woodland, we arrived at the porter's lodge, which is about a mile from the Washington mansion. Handing some silver to the old black woman, who here opened the gate for us, we proceeded, under the shade of venerable oaks, along the path, which Washington had often traveled before us. The air, as it undulated through the dim aisles of the forest, was cool and refreshing. Spring was fast weaving for the trees a thick mantle of green. I was surprised at the many beautiful birds, which were on the wing. The blue-jay, the red-headed woodpecker, and the king-fisher were among the most conspicuous. We soon began to catch glimpses of the Potomac, as, heaving and falling, it glittered through the intervening foliage. After passing a range of low buildings, the habitations of the slaves, we approached the main edifice, and, consigning our horse to the care of a little black fellow, entered the gate. . . .

We went in search of the grave. Some willows on the side of the bank attracted our attention. They once waved over the remains of Washington; but the tomb has been lately removed to a spot selected by himself. A square front of freestone, enclosing an iron gate, marks the entrance of the spot where he reposes. A few cedar-trees are scattered around, and the top of the sepulchre is covered with earth and with decaying brambles. Standing over the dust of Washington, an American must ever feel deeply the impressiveness of the occasion, whatever may be the associations and the scenes around him. The Father of his Country needs no haughty mausoleum, towering above his ashes, to perpetuate his memory,

> "Nor that his hallowed reliques should be hid
> Under a starry-pointing pyramid."

But I would have every thing about the spot of his long home in harmony with the emotions, which must be awakened in the bosom of the pilgrim who visits it. I would remove every unsightly object, deracinate the weeds and briers, which now offend the eye, clear away the rubbish, which has collected around the place, and let the crisp turf cover it, so that,

Until regular steamboat service from Washington, D.C., and Alexandria was established in the 1850s, most visitors entered the estate on the land side of the mansion, through the entrance-way sketched by Benson J. Lossing for his *Mount Vernon and Its Associations: Historical, Biographical, and Pictorial* (1859). Typically an elderly African American man stationed at the gate houses admitted visitors to the property. (Courtesy of Special Collections, University of Virginia Library)

"When Spring, with dewy fingers cold,
Returns to deck the hallowed mould,
She then shall dress a sweeter sod
Fancy's feet have ever trod."

It is said, that, at the time Lafayette visited the grave of Washington, in 1825 [1824], an eagle, one which might have been a fit model for our country's emblem, kept hovering over the spot, as long as our country's guest remained there. On his departure, the noble bird rose proudly into the air, then swept downward and disappeared in the thick covert of woods, which skirt the shore.

We silently quitted the burial-place, and, in a few minutes, entered the summer-house on the brow of the Mount. The structure is of wood, and is rapidly falling to decay. It is covered with the names and the initials of numerous visiters, who seem to have hoped to achieve immortality by the aid of their penknives. As we sat, following with our glance the wake of a steam-boat, which had rushed vaporing by a moment before, an old white-headed negro approached us and withdrew our attention. His name, he told us, was Oliver Smith, and he had once been in the service of Washington. He seemed to entertain a lively and grateful recollection of his old master. He was present when Washington dismounted from his horse for the last time. The weather had been raw and stormy, and the cold sleet had fallen down his neck. An inflammation of the throat ensued, and the next evening the hero of Mount Vernon breathed his last. Our informant told us that Washington used to be uniformly kind in his language and manner towards him, and that he never heard him utter an oath, even when he had cause for irritation. He was accustomed to retire regularly to bed at ten o'clock, and to rise before the sun, and on horseback, make the circuit of his estate. He took a great deal of exercise, and his constitution demanded it. On Sundays, he would attend church at Alexandria. He was rarely seen to smile by his domestics. He was methodical in his habits, and remarkable for his love of neatness and of order. These statements only confirm what has been said of him before. Before quitting Mount Vernon, we visited the garden, and found that it did not bear those appearances of neglect, which I regretted to perceive in other parts of the estate. The hot-house contained some flourishing orange-trees; and a variety of rare flowers lined the well-graveled walks.

A train of dark clouds, rolling up from the horizon, now warned us to depart; and, leaving some memorials of our visit with old Oliver Smith, who, by the way, is a sound Whig, and sticks to the principles of his world-revered master, we bade adieu to the spot, with which so many stirring associations are connected.

1839
"I WAS NEVER MORE DISAPPOINTED IN MY LIFE"
L. Osgood

The following description emphasizes deterioration, even of the new tomb. Wide dissemination of this kind of information raised public concern about the eventual fate of the site, as well as conviction that it must be preserved. These developments preceded any organized historic preservation movement in the United States. During the late 1840s this movement began with a national petitioning campaign aimed at pressuring the United States Congress to purchase Mount Vernon on behalf of the American people.

This depiction appears in L. Osgood's "Visit to Mount Vernon, 1839." It is among the holdings of the Mount Vernon Ladies' Association and is used with permission.

Written at Washington DC
  June 28th 1839

  Mt Vernon in 1839 by a Native of this Country

Thinking that a day spent in the country, to enjoy the pure air, and a pleasant ride would enliven my health and spirits I lately set my face towards Mt. Vernon. . . . But I am under the disagreeable necessity of saying I was never more disappointed in my life, than on this visit. The home of Washington in life. His resting place in death, the most hallowed spot in America's soul and a place visited yearly by thousands should be suffered to moulder and decay apparently with its once illustrious possessor.

The Mansion is in much the best repair of any [of] the buildings but its noble piazza at the eastern front has already borrowed two natural columns from the forest, to support that which was once supported by columns wrought by the hand of the artist.

. . . The rooms are very high and airy and cannot be otherwise than a most delightful summer residence being surrounded by trees of the forest at a short distance from the buildings and cultivated trees near the Mansion and other buildings.

Four years ago one of the green houses was destroyed by fire and one quarter of the black walls are still standing to point out to the stranger what has been. At this fire the greater part of the plants, flowers, and shrubbery were destroyed, which like the buildings have never been restored and the present stock is small. There is a lemon tree upwards of fifty years of age planted by the hand of Washington from which I procured a lemon as a token of him that planted the tree.

The out buildings are all built of brick but they are in a deplorable condition, some that are unoccupied have neither doors or windows but the

152

When L. Osgood visited the estate in 1839, he was surprised and saddened at the deteriorating condition of buildings and grounds. The greenhouse and slave quarter complex had burned a few years earlier, and the ruins would stand for many more years. Between the ruins and the mansion (the most distant building in this undated photograph) lay one of Mount Vernon's famous gardens. (Courtesy of the Mount Vernon Ladies' Association)

walls and shattered roof are left to tell the stranger what has been and buildings that were occupied needed the hand of the carpenter and glazier to give them a healthful appearance.

The garden that only required but the ordinary manual labor was only cultivated in part. By the side of the principal walks, and at the end where the strawberry bed was located the weeds were kept down, but at the back of the garden nothing but weeds were to be seen, but in perfect keeping with things around it.

Eastman Johnson's 1857 painting of the interior of the kitchen, located
near the mansion, poignantly captures the decline of the estate and the
conditions in which its African American inhabitants lived.
(Courtesy of the Mount Vernon Ladies' Association)

The old gardner seemed very proud of once belonging to Washington
and took more interest in talking of his former gardening than exhibiting the present as well he might.[1] He offered me some cherries he had
gathered and seating myself in the shade I soon made way with them.
They were the largest & best cherries I had seen in a long time. I gave the
old servant a quarter for his lemon and cherries and left him to his
reflections.

The present family in the occupancy is the widow of the late John
Washington a nephew of the Gen.[2] I did not see any of the family as they
ocupied the upper part of the house but I saw a splendid full length portrait of the family consisting of Mrs Washington one son & two daughters. This most splendid painting was by Chapman.[3] . . .

The Tomb also is in a delapidated condition.

Because of difficulties with the new tomb constructed in the early 1830s,
the remains of George and Martha Washington were removed and placed in
marble sarcophagi brought from Philadelphia. To accommodate them, a larger,
brick enclosure was constructed. Until it was ready, the sarcophagi were stored
in the yard. Russell Smith painted the enlarged new tomb about 1839.
(Courtesy of the Mount Vernon Ladies' Association)

The two sarcophaguses are placed in wooden boxes or pens placed
without the vault in the enclosed yard. The vault is very damp, and a kind
of acid is produced by water leaking through the bricks and mortar is so
powerful as to rot mahogany boards in three years, and two Gentlemen
from Philadelphia Strickland an Architect and the Gentleman that
manufactured the sarcophagus of Washington when they took it to Mt
Vernon and discovered the state of the vault they said the acid would dis-
solve the marble in seven years and in consequence of this unfortunate

circumstance the sarcophagus are cooped in the open yard and hid from the eye of the Visitor.[4]

At the Tomb I found Maj. Lewis Washington[5] a cousin of the Gen. who resides on a farm about four miles from Mt. Vernon.

He had taken upon himself the trouble & expense of repairing the Tomb being one of the nearest of the relatives living and probably took as deep an interest in the preservation of those sacred remains as if he had the ocupancy and possesion of Mt. Vernon himself.

He had his own servants there at work preparing for the Masons, who will put a new arch to the vault laid in hydraulic cement.

The wall that encloses the vault is very bad. The materials used for mortar appear to have been but little else than sand. The rain has washed out the mortar and left the top bricks loose and also greatly damaged both sides of the vault.

Boys have clim[b]ed over the wall to get a peep at the sarcophagus and have tumbled down many of the loose bricks from the top of the wall.

1. Phil, the gardener, apparently mimicked his father, Oliver Smith, in claiming to have been a slave of GW.

2. John Augustine Washington (d. 1832) was the nephew of Bushrod Washington, not GW.

3. Osgood erred. The John Gadsby Chapman painting shows Jane C. Washington with her daughter Anna Maria and sons Richard Blackburn and John Augustine Washington (see the illustration on p. 137).

4. In 1837 the architect William Strickland designed a marble sarcophagus for the remains of GW, which stonemason John Struthers voluntarily constructed. When the two men traveled from Philadelphia to Mount Vernon that September, they discovered that the door of the new tomb was too small to admit the sarcophagus and, in any event, the vault was unsuitable for it. Therefore the sarcophagus was crated and placed nearby while an enclosure in front of the tomb was constructed. Osgood saw the site in this condition, by which time a second sarcophagus, for Martha Washington, also awaited final installation.

5. Lawrence Lewis of Woodlawn, GW's nephew and last surviving executor of his estate.

1840

An Inheritance Shared with the Nation
Jane Charlotte Washington

As owner of the estate, Jane C. Washington was especially conscious of the toll that time, weather, and thousands of visitors were taking on the buildings and grounds. In this letter to a kinsman, she advanced the idea of a federal appropriation to assist the family in maintaining what had long since become a de facto national site. Here, too, she voiced deep conviction that pilgrimages to Mount Vernon contributed to the well-being of the nation.

This letter, dated 25 May, to George Corbin Washington is among the holdings of the Mount Vernon Ladies' Association and is used with permission.

For myself and children personally my dear Cousin I do not desire, nor have we any right to expect, any favours from the General Government, but such as are bestowed on any other individuals of our Country. We are unwilling to sell our inheritance here, yet as the Nation already shares it with us, a common sense of justice would I think point out the necessity of an appropriation, unsolicited on our part, and respectfully tendered, to enable *us* to keep up the improvements, and meet the expences we are daily subjected to by the publick.

I never would have submitted to the endless intrusions, and sacrifice of every thing like private right and domestic privacy to which we are liable here, but that I believe it arises frequently from a sincere (though thoughtlessly indulged) desire of honouring the memory of Genl. Washington. 'Tis a feeling calculated to inspire and strengthen virtuous and patriotic principles, and cement more firmly the ties, that bind us together as a Nation. We have done, and shall continue to do all we can to keep the place from intire decay. It is yearly becoming more expensive and difficult to do so; the buildings all ought to be thoroughly repaired, or they must in a few years go down—when that occurs, if unable to do better, I trust the family will erect a 'Log Cabin,' and still let the place descend to the Name and family of Washington. A family I must say, whose simple integrity of heart, disinterested honesty of purpose, and pure patriotism, must ever make worthy the Inheritance.

1840
"MARKED AND SCRATCHED ALL OVER"
Robert W. Nelson

On a hot summer's day in 1840, boys from the recently founded Episcopal high school near Alexandria walked all the way to Mount Vernon in the company of a teacher. This diary entry, written by one of the students, tells as much of the journey as of the destination.

This entry for 16 July is in the Robert W. Nelson Commonplace Book, in the Francis K. Nelson Farm Diary, a copy of which is housed in Special Collections at the University of Virginia Library, Charlottesville; it is used with permission.

Thursday July 16th, 1840. I arose this morning very early (about day break) and after making an hearty breakfast on bread and butter, set out with Six other Students of the High School, and our worthy professor of Aincient Languages, for Mount Vernon once the count[r]y seat of

General George Washington about ten miles distant from Howard.[1] It was a fine day for an excursion of this kind, but the foreruners of Excessive heat were visable, which afterwards proved to be strictly true. We proceeded on our way some what in a southeasterly direction following the course of the Potomac. After having walked about 3 or 4 miles we came to the house of a gray haired friend, one who in his youthfull days had been my Mothers instucter in Music. After having rested ourselves sufficiently we again set out, taking the son of the old gentleman as a guid[e]. We then walked across two or three Old fields, until we reached the road leading from Alexandria to Mount Vernon. After walking a little fa[r]ther we came to a spring near the road side where we stoped to refresh ourselves. As for myself I was very glad of the opportunity to rest for being out of the habit of walking I was a good deal fatigued. I now began to repent my undertaking the walk, but as I was being much cheered up and encouraged by our Profr. we proceeded on our road, and here let me remark that but for the jokes and cheering spirits of amiable profs. we would not have undertaken the trip, and if we had, we would certainly have given up on the road.

After gowing on about two miles we stopped again and after having refreshed with cool well water we proceeded on our way and did not stop again untill we reached Mt. Vernon. This was the longest stretch we had during the day. At last we entered the gate that opened into a beautiful Wood once the park [of] General Washington. On either side of the gate were small houses, very much resembling some old porters lodge on the borders of an English Baron's estate. The road from this place to the House was very romantic, and I almost fancied myself in one of those glens which are so beautifully described by Mr. Sherwood in Roxabell. We Meandered through a very pretty glen untill we reached [the] house where we sat dow[n] to rest from the fatigue of the journ[e]y. After a while we arose to look about the premises. We first went in front of the house which is about eighty or ninety feet long and two stories high. A porch from the ground to the eves of those extended the whole length of the building. The house is bui[l]t of wood with squar[e] blocks of wood nailed over the Weather boarding, giving it so much the appearance of a stone house that I at first took it for one. Being then quite hungry we walked around to the kitchen in quest of food; luckely for us the Milk Maid had just finished Churning. Each of us then drank about a half pint of Buttermilk for which we paid three times as much as it was worth, but we were very thankful to get it at allmost any price. We then went into the summer house which was marked and scratched all over with names, but as I did not care to clas[s] myself with such a vulgar crowd I let it alone. I then went on down to the old tomb of Washington which is built of sandstone so very soft that you might almost crush it with your hand. Owing to this circumstance a year or two since the Bones of the general were moved into a new tomb buil[t] by one of [crossed out: the picadillos of Washington]. We then went down to the new tomb which was built of brick. It was quite a pretty one but not enough so for the Father of our country.

1. An earlier name for the school.

1841
A RARE OPPORTUNITY
M****

Except during the winter months, about fifty pilgrims arrived each day during the 1840s. Most strolled the grounds but were not allowed into the mansion. Admittance there required a proper letter of introduction. One rainy June day, however, Jane C. Washington made an exception and personally entertained strangers. With her was her eldest son, twenty-year-old John Augustine Washington, whom she was preparing to take over management of the estate.

This account appeared in M****, "A Visit to the Birthplace and to the Tomb of Washington," *Daily National Intelligencer* (Washington, D.C.), 29 June 1841.

To visit Mount Vernon still remained; so, on the 21st, I took the steamboat, and at 4 o'clock P.M. arrived at Alexandria and stopped at the Marshall House. Early on the following Monday a carriage was in readiness, and we set out for Mount Vernon in a party of four. It was cloudy, and ere we proceeded far, rain began to fall. Having reached the premises of the venerated place, we alighted; a slow pace brought us within sight of the enclosure where the mortal remains lie of him who "is first in the hearts of his countrymen." In descending the declivity which leads to it we were joined by others; the gentlemen's heads were simultaneously uncovered—not a word was spoken—we approached the gratings, and, with hearts filled with veneration, looked in upon the silent mansion of the illustrious dead. Within the enclosure there are two sarcophagi. The one to the right covers the ashes of the virtuous and the great, and upon it are sculptured the eagle and other national emblems. An inscription in small characters at its foot declares it to be the gift of John Struthers with the permission of Lawrence Lewis, the surviving executor; the one on the left is that of his deceased lady, and is adorned with the following chaste and eloquent epitaph:

MARTHA, the consort

OF

WASHINGTON.

After some minutes our silence had a pause, and the conversation which followed was characterized by the solemnity which the occasion required. The rain continued to fall; we retired under an adjoining tree for shelter. We were not there long when a servant came with the compliments of Mrs. Jane [C.] Washington and an invitation to walk up to the house. It was thankfully accepted; we sent our cards by the bearer. We followed, and were received by her eldest son with the characteristic ease and good breeding of a gentleman. Mrs. Washington soon made her appearance, and, concluding from the extreme paleness and apparent fatigue of one of the ladies of the party that her health was delicate, she kindly prevailed on her to retire and lie down, telling her "to consider herself at home, for she was in the house of an old Christian." She retired, and experienced as much attention and tenderness as if she were under her maternal roof.

The Key of the Bastile, which was sent by Lafayette to General WASHINGTON, hangs suspended in a small glass-case in the hall. As I looked at it and thought of the Bastile, I was seized by a momentary terror mixed with detestation. What scenes of human wo[e] presented themselves to my imagination! The Bastile was levelled with the ground —its royal master beheaded—revolutionary France was inundated with an ocean of blood, and the world saw the empire of an hour floating on its surface, and saw it go down forever—the Bourbons were restored— the ill-fated Bourbons. Where are they now? But, alas! what has been the fate of European liberty?

With such reflections as these I turned away, and went out into the portico, and looked down on the placid surface of the Potomac. Refreshments were brought and partaken of. Here we were joined by Mr. J. [A.] WASHINGTON, who answered my numerous interrogations concerning his immortal relative with great affability. We sat down where the father of his country was wont to sit, in the full enjoyment of repose,

John Augustine Washington (1821–61), the last private owner of Mount Vernon.
(Photograph, 1861, courtesy of the Mount Vernon Ladies' Association)

when his great work was finished—the freeing of his country—to contemplate her future greatness.

Subsequently we were shown through the parlors and library; many curiosities and objects of interest to the patriot were pointed out to us. I had the gratification to perceive that the family were pleased with my visit to the *birthplace*,[1] and was honored by being presented by Mrs. J. [C.] WASHINGTON, in the hall of *Mount Vernon* house, with a cane that grew on the tomb of the most illustrious of American citizens. Meanwhile visiters continued to pour in, and we, having taken our leave, departed—happy for having gone there with motives so laudable, and deeply impressed with gratitude for the mode of our reception.

1. GW's birthplace on Pope's Creek, in Westmoreland County, Virginia.

1842

THE NEW PROPRIETOR
John Augustine Washington

"Worn out" by the flow of visitors, who "consider me one of the curiosities of the place," Jane C. Washington was eager to place Mount Vernon in the hands of her son John. Shortly after he came of age in 1842, she agreed to lease him the land and twenty-one slaves in return for five hundred dollars annually. He thereby became the first nineteenth-century proprietor to have lived much of his childhood at the estate. Considering his new status, John's reception at the mansion at Christmastime 1842 seemed entirely inappropriate. This letter is addressed to his future wife, Eleanor Love Selden, of Leesburg, Virginia.

This letter, dated 29 December, is among the holdings of the Mount Vernon Ladies' Association and is used with permission. The material quoted above is found in a 28 June 1837 letter from Jane C. Washington to her sons, Christian and John; it is also used with permission of the MVLA.

I did not arrive here until very late in the evening of Christmas day, and shall not very easily forget my reception, which was gloomy and provoking enough to me at the time, but would no doubt have been highly amusing to an unconcerned spectator. Before dismounting I called loudly to the servant who usually attends me, but receiving no answer, I screamed at the top of my voice first for one and then another until I had invoked the assistance of all, even old women and children. But the deserted walls scarcely gave an echo to my cries; and there I was, presenting the singular spectacle, of a gentleman (without any apparent cause) sitting on horseback before his own door at a late hour of the evening, having screamed himself so hoarse as to be almost unable to speak any longer, still looking about as if he felt very queer, but did not know exactly what to do, and at last finding himself in that awkward predicament described in scripture, as "having called aloud but there was none to answer and looked around but there was none to help." I had almost given up in despair when I heard a Singular sound like a heavy log rolling leisurely down a long stairway, and a boy emerged from one of the doors, and after looking at the top of the house and in other directions where no one could by any possibility have been, he at last got the right one, and discovered that someone was calling and who it was. After a series of not mild questions, I had the satisfaction to learn that himself and another boy were the sole occupants. The rest were gone after having securely fastened the doors and windows and hidden the keys where they could not be found, had dispersed themselves in various directions and the interesting youth had not the faintest idea as to when they would return. Very much to my relief however one of them soon got home, and I was enabled to gain admittance, and my thoughts to run back into their favourite channel.

1843

"WITHOUT THINKING THAT WE TRESPASSED"
Caroline Wells Healey

*Twenty-year-old Caroline Wells Healey's remembrance of her visit to
Mount Vernon is more critical than reverential. Her descriptions of
climbing a fence intended to protect the old tomb site, trying to inscribe
her name on the summer house, and pelting hogs with orange peels
during a picnic lunch provide graphic images of public abuse of the
estate. Healey, a Bostonian, also reacted with dismay to seeing slaves
on the property.*

This journal entry for 10 June is among the Caroline Wells Healey Dall Papers,
1811–1917, housed in the Massachusetts Historical Society; it is used with
permission.

About two hours after we left Alexandria we reached Mt. Vernon. We
approached it between two lodges of a yellowish plaster, about ten ft
high, and the gate was opened to us by an old colored woman, wearing a
white cap, who was in the family before the General died and who was
not sorry to feel her fingers close over a piece of money. I should think
the road to the house was at least half a mile long, and in the worst order
possible. It seems as if every stone cried out to the patriotic pilgrim "stay
at home." We approached the house thro' the quarter of the negroes,
which was in better order than those usually attached to plantations in
Virginia. We were making our way to the pump, when a little boy cried
out to us that it was against the rule, which meant I suppose that he
would have been glad of a tip for getting it for us. Passing thro' the clus-
ter of buildings, we saw a strange old blind woman, with a crutch in her

Visitors on the lawn before the mansion are depicted in this
anonymous nineteenth-century engraving.
(Courtesy of the Alexandria Library, Special Collections, Alexandria, Va.)

hand, sitting outside a door. Slaves on the estate of Washington!! She did
not speak to us, and my heart was so full that I could not speak to her.
... We crossed the circular grass plot which is contained in the area, and
by a narrow lane, passed towards the new Tomb. We gathered a few
thorns from the honey locust as we passed along without thinking that
we trespassed. . . . I could not gaze upon this c[e]aselessly, as my companions seemed to do, so I stole away, and was on my return before they
knew it.

We climbed a fence, in order to reach the old tomb, now nothing but
a loose arch whose entrance is choked with rolling stones. Its position is
far more beautiful than that of the new, which is unbosomed in trees. It
commands the river and could be seen by boats passing up and down. A

little higher on the Hill, is the summer house, which is open, and might have been begun in 1492, but has never been finished. Here patriotic visitors inscribe their names and here Giles Scroggins and Gertrude Heindale rest side by side. I wished to make a trio to be handed down to posterity, & in seeking the means, found that I had lost the point of my gold pencil. . . .

We now approached the house in front. . . . We paused a moment, on the portico, within reach of the hospitality of a pair of long settees, when a young servant girl, doubtless commissioned by the higher powers, came to shut the door in our face. Mr Brown handed her the letter, which Judge Cranch had given us to Mrs Washington. She retreated with it, and I saw that she entered the room before which we stood, and upon the sill of whose half open window, rested a plate of fruit. In a few moments she returned and admitted us to the rooms upon the first floor. . . .

From the house we went to the garden and greenhouses. . . . The exotics are not many, but quite beautiful. There was among them . . . an orange tree planted by General Washington's own hand, which bore fruit before his death, and does so still. The garden was laid out, like all gardens in this neighborhood with stiff box[wood] hedges. It was very pretty but neglected. The gardener was the most interesting person we saw on the estate. His hair was white, he has been there, 41 years, and was brought by Bushrod Washington . . . after the General's Death when he went to take possession. He *studied*, as he termed it, with the gardener who originally laid out the grounds. . . .

When we crossed his hand he muttered out his thanks, and we left him to seek a place for our pic nic. He said in answer to an enquiry from me, that there were 30 negroes on the place, a dozen of them hired—the rest owned by Mrs. Washington. We found a shady spot and succeeded in getting a little refreshment, by pelting the hogs with orange peel, which we ate.

1844

"A VOICE NOW CALLS, WHICH SHOULD TOUCH A RESPONSIVE
CHORD IN EVERY HEART"
From the *Democratic Union*

*With increasing frequency travelers' writings included criticism of
Americans for neglecting to halt—indeed, hastening—deterioration of the
estate. Washington family members also received rebuke for the way they
managed their own property. For example, although the plantation had
depended on slave labor since its founding in the seventeenth century,
some observers now voiced exasperation that chattel slavery was allowed
to persist there. As public discourse grew more possessive, customary
small payments for guides' services, as well as charges levied for fruit and
other items, also received censure.*

This traveler's account appeared in "Mount Vernon," *Democratic Union*
(Harrisburg, Pa.), 27 November 1844.

A visit to this hallowed shrine of patriotism and virtue, must ever be
regarded by our countrymen as a duty of the most interesting and impressive character. We had lately an opportunity of embracing the privilege.
... Much injury has been wantonly done to the grounds of Mount Vernon
by shameless persons, and visitors are now obliged to procure a suitable
letter as a voucher for their character, to obtain admittance.

Arrived at the estate, the road leading to the Mansion House, probably half a mile distant, is in such neglected condition, that after several
attempts to proceed in the carriage, we left the vehicle and continued on
foot. The estate is bounded by a forrest composed of venerable trees, the
ground gradually elevated as we proceeded; winding and sequestered

paths are traced through the opening foliage, and an entire separation from the outward world is every where apparent. Continuing leisurely our way we approached a field in which reapers were gathering the harvest, and on asking where Mr. Washington was to be found, were answered by a young man with coat off and rake in hand, who informed us that he answered to the person for whom we enquired. Not a little surprised at the unexpected meeting, we presented our letter and readily accepted an invitation to walk to the house. Mr. John Augustine Washington, a young man about 25 years of age, and the present occupant of the estate of Mount Vernon, is the grand nephew of his great ancestor,[1] and we believe the nearest living connection. . . .

We were first shown into the Library formerly belonging to Washington; it is composed of works in various languages, generally on historical subjects. This room contains the bust of Washington, modelled from life by Houdon; also an engraving of Louis XVI which was presented by the monarch to Washington, at the time our first treaty was made with France. The engraving is a splendid specimen of the art, and is believed to be the only one now in existence; the plate and the impressions having been destroyed during the French Revolution. It is enclosed in a frame embellished with the arms of Louis and Washington. The dining hall of the mansion is a spacious and hospitable looking apartment. Here we saw the picture and key of the Bastile, which were sent to Washington by Lafayette, in 1790, as an "early trophy of the spoils of despotism, and the first ripe fruits of American principles transplanted into Europe." . . .

We were subsequently shown the various other apartments of the Mansion, all of which betoken that air of comfort and convenience which generally characterize the dwellings of our fathers. The room where Washington died, still occupied as a bed-chamber, possesses an interest to be experienced only in pausing before those walls which heard his last words, and in expressive silence responded to the parting spirit.

We have wandered through the house, admired its antique and beautiful cornices, stopped to behold each relic of that majestic form which was wont to linger in these very halls, and stepping out into the verdant lawn, we wonder at the placid serenity which even the atmosphere seems to possess, and inquire for the tomb of Washington. Following a sequestered path, we soon entered a grove shaded with elms and honey-locusts, Washington's favorite tree, and arriving at a plain structure of brick, beheld the tomb. On a tablet over the entrance is the following inscription:

Within this Enclosure

Rest

THE REMAINS OF

GEN. GEORGE WASHINGTON

Through an iron gate is seen a marble sarcophagus containing his ashes, inscribed with the arms of his country, and with eloquent simplicity for an epitaph, the name of

WASHINGTON.

At his side in a corresponding tomb repose the remains of Martha, his beloved wife. The structure containing these precious relics is comparatively new, it having been built in place of the old vault which has fallen in decay; a few withered cedars and a pile of unsightly stones, now mark the spot where reposed the remains of Washington until within a few years.

It is surely not strange if the tomb of departed and virtuous greatness, raises in the mind emotions of a chastening nature, and in pausing at the grave of Washington, may not such feeling be usefully indulged! Here no ordinary thoughts can enter, no earthly longings of a sordid mind; but partaking in the "sacred calm," that

"Bids every fierce tumultuous passion cease,"

we may imbibe an essence of that heaven-born patriotism which so endears the spirit we reverence. While reflecting on the holy teachings of his life, and knowing how often they are forgotten and neglected; that principles are replaced by interest, or lost in the maze of party strife or rancor, it is difficult indeed to reconcile our actions with the dictates of his precepts and example.

The garden of Washington, so much his pride and pleasure, is still to be seen and is yet very beautiful. We were shown several fruit trees planted by the General, which still preserve a hardy vigor. We were accompanied by an old colored man attached to the premises, who offered to sell us any of the plants we desired. A fine specimen of the sago-palm was offered for seven dollars! We were however, contented with purchasing a few lemons from a venerable tree, as mementoes of our visit, and need we add were shocked to learn how easily that garden might be stripped of the last remnant of its beauty. What a reproof, we thought, for ourselves and our country!

The present estate of Mount Vernon comprises about 1200 acres, a comparatively small portion of which is under cultivation, though the land is well adapted for raising various kinds of grain, and we were shown in the Mansion a sheaf of wheat of unusual size and excellence, which had just been gathered from the farm.

Allusion has been made to the key to the Bastille. It will probably surprise some of our readers to learn that this interesting relic was once sold for 75 cents! After the decease of Washington, his effects were exposed to the highest bidder, and of course became the possession of different

Visitors were especially pleased to discover plants that had been growing in the gardens since the time of George and Martha Washington. Some eagerly bought fruit or carried away twigs as mementos, while others considered such souvenir hunting a travesty. Benson J. Lossing's "Century Plant and Lemon-Tree" appeared in *Mount Vernon and Its Associations: Historical, Biographical, and Pictorial* in 1859. (Courtesy of Special Collections, University of Virginia Library)

persons. The key of the Bastille was purchased by Col. Alexander Rind, of Alexandria, who subsequently presented it to the family of Washington; and it is owing to his kind appreciation and generosity that the visitor at Mount Vernon is now shown the gift of La Fayette. . . .[2]

The truth is unacceptable; but its painfulness must not blind our senses to the fact, of the thoughtlessness of his countrymen to Washington, in the unaccountable neglect which has been manifested towards

173

his property and his ashes. Let us look to facts. The very tomb in which his ashes moulder, is the private gift of a stone cutter in Philadelphia; the halls in which he dwelt and where he died, may soon be exposed to the elements, for decay long since has marked the traces of its progress; the garden where he was wont to greet the rising sun, and to offer his grateful orisons, has become a bazar for the sale of his favorite exotics; his farm is half a wilderness, and tilled by slaves who toil in wretched mockery of the spirit that gave freedom to his country!

No American can visit Mount Vernon without feelings deeply humiliating, and from those consecrated shades a voice now calls, which should touch a responsive chord in every heart, and echoing throughout the land, should rouse his countrymen to ordain as a National Inheritance the tomb of Washington, and to cause the spot which he selected from the earth to be his home, worthy of the country to which he gave the legacy of freedom and of the nation who enjoy the fruits of his labors.

1. This attribution is incorrect. John Augustine Washington (d. 1832), who was the husband of Jane C. Washington and father of the young proprietor encountered at Mount Vernon in 1844, was the grandnephew of GW.

2. This story is apocryphal. I am indebted to Mary V. Thompson of MVLA for helping me reach this conclusion.

1846

Preserve This "Landmark on the Highway of Human Freedom"
Samuel I. Prime

More than most written accounts that have survived, the Reverend Samuel Prime's articulates the aura of sacredness that people imparted to the estate and of closeness to the living Washington. Prime and his travel-

*ing companion happened to visit on a day when Jane C. Washington was
present, and she ushered them through the house then occupied by John
Augustine Washington and his family. In publishing this account in a
New York newspaper, Prime helped disseminate Jane's view that the federal government should purchase and preserve Mount Vernon.*

This portrayal appeared in Samuel I. Prime's "A Pilgrimage to the Tomb of
Washington," *New-York Observer* (New York City), 27 June 1846.

My companion in travel was an elderly clergyman who when a boy had
seen the living Washington, and now joined me in a journey of filial piety
to the grave of "the Father of his Country." After a toilsome ride of two
hours through a country that had nothing to interest us beyond the fact
that Washington had so often traversed it, we reached the gate of Mount
Vernon about noon. An old female servant tottered from the lodge on a
staff to the gate to open it, and in answer to our inquires, told us that she
was in the family when George Washington died. It was grateful to find
one link, though such an one, between the illustrious dead and the living. Entering the gate we were at once on consecrated ground. The carriage way, sufficiently rough to intimate that no facilities are afforded to
visitors, winds through an ancient woodland; and the great trees, solemn
and silent seemed to speak of the man who had preferred their shadows
to the sunshine of courts. These were the shades of Mount Vernon, and
soon we reached the mansion, on the banks of the Potomac, with a green
lawn sloping to the river in front and gardens in the rear. It was indeed
a fitting place for one no more a hero than a sage! A simple two-story
house, with columns in front, and lodges for servants running back from
each end of it, it would appear to be the private residence of some country gentleman of moderate means; and it was difficult to believe that this
had been the resort of the most distinguished men of our own country

and of the friends of liberty from other lands, who have here sought the shrine at which Washington [is] worshipped.

During the eight years that he was devoted to the service of his country in the tented field, Washington never visited Mount Vernon but once, and then accidentally as he was on his way to Yorktown with Count De Rochambeau; and we must see the spot and know the tastes and private habits of the man, before we are able to appreciate the sacrifice he made in leaving this retreat for the turmoils of the camp and the toils of state. . . .

Here were the solitary walks and paths of private life which the footsteps of the great man pressed; *here* he rested when wearied with labour in the field; *these* trees he planted with his own hands, and the [trees] from which *these* [flowers] sprung were [of] his own training in the morning and the evening of his wonderful life.

But we must knock at the door of his house. The door stones have been lying here half a century, and we are standing where he has often stood to look upon the grounds that he loved. The throng of visitors is so constant and great, that it is necessary for the protection of the house, to admit no strangers but those who bring private letters of introduction to the family, and we were so well provided in this respect, that we met with no delay. Mrs. Washington, a lady venerable in years and worth, received us in the library of the General, a sacred room, which has been preserved as nearly as possible in the state in which he left it. Here were several family pictures, and various memorials of the great man: the original bust by Houdon placed over the door by Washington's own hand, and never since removed: here were the books that he was fond of perusing, and with emotion I took down from the shelf the old family Bible that he used, and looked at *his* autograph *there*. I should be glad to own *that* autograph of Washington! I would bequeath it and the Bible as a rich legacy to my children. The Father of his country loved his Bible.

176

The library. (Photograph, 1998, by Robert C. Lautman,
courtesy of the Mount Vernon Ladies' Association)

Mrs. Washington had welcomed us with a cordiality that we had no right to anticipate, but her feeble health constrained us to beg that she would now commit us to the guide of a servant through the house, but with great urbanity and kindness she insisted upon being our guide, from room to room, while with earnest but gentle dignity she pointed out the various memorials of the man which were constantly meeting the eye. . . .

The chamber where the good man breathed his last is on the second story in the South West corner, and is now the private room of the lady of the house: sacred, as it should be, against public intrusion. . . .

. . . Other men may have been greater and better as statesmen, warriors, philosphers or christians, but there was in Washington such a symmetrical development of all the qualities that ennoble the man and make him the ornament of his race, that his chracter stands out on the page of time as a standard of excellence, not to be envied but imitated and admired.

It was a solemn place to stand upon that turf by the tomb of Washington. We felt it so. The memory of the illustrious dead was precious there, and it was good to dwell upon it. Leaving the sepulchre we went through the gardens which he had laid out and the conservatory where the orange trees which he had planted were bearing fruit, and having received a few plants that are now adorning another and distant spot, we prepared to bid adieu to Mount Vernon.

I cannot refrain from saying here that the Government ought to become the proprietor of these acres. The incessant and increasing stream of strangers renders it undesirable as a place of private residence, but its gates ought never to be closed against the pilgrims who travel hither to see where Washington lived and died and is buried. Hundreds of years hence, and thousands if the world stands, though the Union be dissolved and the Republic of Washington find a tomb among the sepulchres of nations, yet so long as one lover of liberty lives among men, the spot where Washington lies will be precious to his heart, and he will desire to make a pilgrimage thither. When a hundred millions of people are within the area of these states—our children's children will be a part of them—each and every one of that vast multitude of people will have the same interest in the name of Washington that *we* have; they will know him, and love him as well as we do; thousands of them will every year make the tour to Mount Vernon, and go back to tell their children that they have been to the tomb of Washington; and other thousands will come from other lands; and more as other lands are illumined and made free by the power of *his* principles and example; and believing as we do that the genius of our institutions is yet to pervade the earth as the gospel establishes the rights of man, the day may come when the grave of the great Apostle of liberty will be the most illustrious landmark on the highway of human freedom. Our government therefore ought to purchase it: protect it against lawless intrusion: provide facilities for access to the mount by water: preserve the house and grounds, as nearly as may be, in their present condition, and thus transmit to posterity the legacy that belongs to the future. A very moderate "pilgrim tax" would meet all the expenses, and a revenue would eventually accrue which might be appropriated to carry out a munificent scheme of education which Washington devised, and for the promotion of which he bequeathed a sum of money which is now on interest, and is to be applied to the object when it shall have reached an adequate amount.[1] I would urge the attention of our public men to this subject, were it not too true that we have few public men who have any tendencies toward works whose results are to be seen and felt in the ideal and moral only. If we should urge that a rail road from Washington to Mount Vernon would furnish a good investment, there are men, enough of them, who would listen to the project and estimate the profits: but to propose the purchase of Mount Vernon to illustrate the Nation's love of the Nation's Father, and to be a shrine for the friends of liberty of all lands and times, finds no response in the minds of great men of our day. They were not made great men for that. Yet it should be done, and that speedily.

I shall ever cherish with peculiar emotions the memory of my visit to Mount Vernon. The simple but elegant manners of the venerable Mrs. Washington, the mother of the present proprietor; her attentions and hospitality, will be remembered, and the impressions of the hours that I passed at the mansion and the grave of him who was "first in peace, first in war, and first in the hearts of his countrymen,"[2] will be among the last that time will efface.

1. An academy at Alexandria, Virginia, and Liberty Hall Academy (later Washington and Lee University) in Rockbridge County received bequests under GW's 1799 will. In addition, he left fifty shares of stock in the Potomac Company, in the hope that they would help endow a university for the District of Columbia.

2. This is a paraphrase of "first in war, first in peace, and first in the hearts of his countrymen," the famous words that originated in General Henry "Light Horse Harry" Lee's oration after GW's death.

1850

AN APPEAL TO THE NORTH AND THE SOUTH
Mrs. C****

*This account coincides with high political tension in the United States, as Congress patched together the famous Compromise of 1850, the last great sectional compromise before the Civil War. Standing before Washington's tomb, "Mrs. C****" envisioned this "sacred spot" as a place where northerners and southerners, inspired by the founder's example, might yet come together and rededicate themselves to preserving the nation.*

Mrs. C****'s account appeared in her "A Visit to Mount Vernon," *Daily National Intelligencer* (Washington, D.C.), 14 June 1850.

I had long wished to make a visit to Mount Vernon, but had been deterred by a reluctance to intrude on the privacy of a family on whom I had no claim but that of being an American and an admirer of WASHINGTON. That reluctance recently gave way before the stronger feeling of attachment to, and a desire to be with and to contribute to the happiness of a valued relative, who was on a visit to me from the "Far West," and who thought his mission would be but half accomplished if he failed to visit the Tomb of Washington. With as much reverence, perhaps with as much devotion, as a Mahometan would visit the shrine of Mecca, did he make this pilgrimage. As he descended the hill leading to the tomb, with uncovered head, his whitened locks spoke of length of years, and the big tears which rolled down his manly furrowed cheeks declared, *He lives "in the hearts of his countrymen."* With a small family party, and those of kindred taste and feeling, I visited this sacred spot. To one of my temperament, to make this excursion with the giddy and the gay would seem almost like sacrilege. As I stood at the tomb, and realized I was near all that remained of that godlike man, I felt most solemnly, most patriotically impressed. Come one, come all, to this sacred spot, and reflect on the self-sacrificing spirit, the patience, the endurance, the firmness, the calmness, the dignity—in a word, the patriotism—of him who was "first in war, first in peace, and first in the hearts of his countrymen." Old as this quotation is, often as it has been used, it can never become stale; its truth, its beauty, give a freshness to it which will never die. It emanated from a head and heart capable of appreciating the transcendant excellencies of WASHINGTON. Ye men of the North, ye men of the South, come, oh! come to this hallowed spot, and, around this sacred sarcophagus, promise to live together like brothers, for he was the Father of you *all*. Strike not one star from that bright galaxy! Tear not one stripe from that broad banner which waves "over the land of the free and the home of the brave." Oh! Let it wave forever, unmutilated, over the sacred mausoleum of him who was prepared to pledge "his life, his fortune, and his sacred honor" to defend it.

A letter of introduction from an honorable Secretary procured us an entrance to the house, where we were most hospitably received by Mr. and Mrs. WASHINGTON.[1] I was quite charmed with the easy grace of the lady, and the frank politeness of the gentleman, and left them grateful for their politeness, and sincerely regretting the embarrassment of their position. While we were there, (two and a half hours,) I witnessed the arrival and departure of six parties, all of whom were admitted to the house. Where is the generosity, the magnanimity, the justice of the American people, that they can permit the Heirs of WASHINGTON, the guardians of his remains, to be taxed and harassed in this manner? Congress, and Congress alone, can remedy this evil. We have no National Monument; we have raised no lofty column; we have carved no storied urn, to perpetuate his memory; and it appears to me we could erect no monument so impressive, none calculated to exert so happy an influence on the moral feelings, as the Residence and the Tomb of WASHINGTON. Then let Congress purchase them, and appoint suitable persons to preserve and protect the property, and act as guides to visitors. I would say, keep the house and grounds, as nearly as possible, consistently with their preservation, as they were in the lifetime of WASHINGTON. Let them tell of the taste, the habits of the man, and of the times in which he lived. It would be a profitable lesson. All modern improvements, I think, would be in bad taste. Being a Lady, I do not presume to discuss the constitutionality of these suggestions; I leave that to wiser heads.[2] I will, however, simply remark, that, as Congress has given large sums for the purchase of pictures,

Eleanor Love Selden Washington (d. 1860), the wife of John Augustine Washington.
This portrait by an unidentified artist is probably posthumous.
(Courtesy of the Mount Vernon Ladies' Association)

statues, and for the support of a national museum, to improve the taste, and impart information to the American people, and has also purchased the papers of distinguished statesmen, I think, under the same clause, and for the same reasons, MOUNT VERNON might be purchased. These suggestions are presented with much diffidence, but my patriotism and sense of justice will not permit me to withhold them.

1. John Augustine Washington and his wife, Eleanor Love Selden Washington. The couple married in 1843.

2. Under the Constitution the state of Virginia would have to agree before any land within its borders could be transferred to the national government. Virginia's unwillingness to see Mount Vernon become federal property meant that Congress never seriously considered purchasing the site.

1850

"The Most Delightful Day of Our Lives"
"Rambler"

"Rambler," who lived in Norfolk, took his daughters along on a journey to the northern part of Virginia, where they passed a day at Mount Vernon. There they met the mulatto West Ford, who had moved to the estate with Bushrod Washington in 1802, subsequently was freed, and remained in the area. By the time "Rambler" and his children encountered Ford, he was employed by John Augustine Washington and on that day was protecting the mansion from intrusion and the relentless relic hunting of souvenir seekers. One member of the party nonetheless managed to make off with a fragment of wood siding.

This portrayal appeared in "A Trip to the Episcopal Convention at Alexandria—Mount Vernon, &c.," by "Rambler," in *Alexandria Gazette and Virginia Advertiser*, 19 June 1850.

We approached the house, and were met by old West Ford, a venerable servant who was born in the Washington family. He informed us, that his master and family had gone to Alexandria, to attend church, and his

"West Ford," from Benson J. Lossing, *Mount Vernon and Its Associations: Historical, Biographical, and Pictorial* (1859).
(Courtesy of Special Collections, University of Virginia Library)

positive instructions were, not to open the house to any person, unless a letter from his master to him, was produced. There was a party present, who had a letter from Mr. Webster[1] to Mr. Washington, and they importuned old West Ford, offering him money to allow them to enter the house: but the old man could not be moved from his integrity:—the gentleman in this party, was a member of Congress from New York.

185

It was a sad disappointment to us pilgrims from afar, not to stand under the roof that sheltered the great Washington, but it was to be borne, and we determined to bear it with the best grace. . . .

. . . Old West Ford offered to conduct us to the Tomb, through the garden, &c., and was ready to tell us all he knew about the old General, but to enter the house, was a thing impossible without a letter from Mr. Washington to him, the said West Ford, instructing him, the said West Ford, to admit the bearer. I fully appreciate the propriety of the interdiction; the family of Mr. Washington has been very much annoyed by visitors during his absence from home, unscrupulous visitors, some of them, who chipped the mantlepieces, and mutilated every thing in their way, in order to provide themselves with mementoes of the place.

I was very much amused with one of my ladies, who coveted a memento of Mount Vernon. She was unable because of her infirmity to roam about as much as the rest of the party. I therefore procured her a comfortable seat, in the great front piazza, and left her to her reflections. In this situation, she observed a small fragment of a board, on the house side, which was nearly detached, bringing away with it the nail that doubtless was driven when the house was built. She very quietly completed the detachment, and pocketed the fragment and the nail, which she produced in the carriage as we rode away, as evidence of the trespass she had committed. . . .

After strolling around the house, looking in at the windows, walking in the great piazza, calling upon our fancy to spread her boldest wing, and bring up before us the long past time, when the illustrious dead peopled the place we were occupying, we took our steps slowly and sadly to the tomb of the illustrious Washington. . . .

. . . There is an iron grating forming the door of the tomb, and the remains of Washington are immediately at the door, so that you can nearly touch the sarcophagus. My little girls brought to Norfolk, sprigs of cedar cut from a tree standing before the door of the tomb, which were cast upon the coffin of Washington and withdrawn.

Old West Ford informed us it was his practice periodically to enter the tomb and brush from the sarcophagus the accumulated leafy offerings with which the loving countrymen of Washington, and pilgrims from distant parts of the earth, literally covered it.

We had the good fortune to be permitted to enter, and walk through the splendid garden, in which Washington took so much pride and pleasure.

. . . The gardener furnished my little girls with beautiful bouquets, composed of flowers, which they religiously preserved and brought with them to Norfolk.

After wearying ourselves with walking and standing—there was so much to see: so much to examine; so much to think about—we selected a lovely spot just in front of the house, immediately on the brow of the high bluff overlooking the majestic Potomac, where we spread our "provant" and ourselves on the green grass, and took our first and last lunch at Mount Vernon. We had nearly spent the most delightful and gratifying day of our lives, and very reluctantly admitted the propriety of taking our departure from Mount Vernon. Soon after we started, our gracious driver, more obsequious because the time drew near when he expected to receive the shining quarter, proposed to drive us to Washington's Spring, where we might obtain a drink of delicious water. The water was indeed beautiful, gushing in a pearly stream from a shaded hill side, and the scene and associations were indeed refreshing and sublime.

1. Senator Daniel Webster.

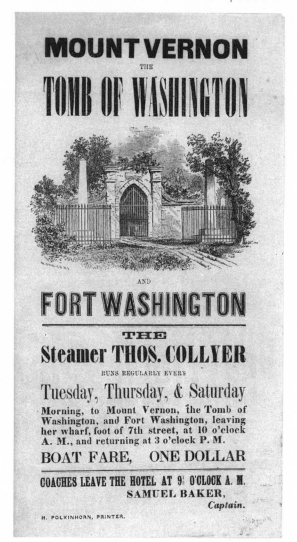

MOUNT VERNON
THE
TOMB OF WASHINGTON

AND

FORT WASHINGTON

THE
Steamer THOS. COLLYER

RUNS REGULARLY EVERY

Tuesday, Thursday, & Saturday

Morning, to Mount Vernon, the Tomb of Washington, and Fort Washington, leaving her wharf, foot of 7th street, at 10 o'clock A. M., and returning at 3 o'clock P. M.

BOAT FARE, ONE DOLLAR

COACHES LEAVE THE HOTEL AT 9½ O'CLOCK A. M.
SAMUEL BAKER,
Captain.

H. POLKINHORN, PRINTER.

Owners of the steamboat *Thomas Collyer* successfully negotiated with John Augustine Washington to establish regularly scheduled excursions to Mount Vernon, beginning in 1850. This handbill was used as an advertisement. (Courtesy of the Library of Congress)

1850

Yielding to the Desires of the Public
From the *New-York Daily Tribune*

*As proprietor, John Augustine Washington was considerably more entre-
preneurial than his predecessors. In 1850 he contracted with the owners of
a new steamboat, the* Thomas Collyer, *for regular excursions to Mount
Vernon, in return for a portion of passengers' ticket fees. With improved
access to the estate available, an estimated ten thousand people annually
journeyed there during the early 1850s.*

On 20 August "Mount Vernon" appeared in the *New-York Daily Tribune* (New
York City).

Mr. Washington, the proprietor of the family home and sepulchre of his
illustrious relative, has so far yielded to the desires of the public as to grant
permission, under certain restrictions, to the proprietors of the steamboat
Thomas Collyer, to land passengers there on three days of each week. The
restrictions relate to the exclusion of a bar, and whatever else may lead to
disorder or any species of impropriety. We understand that these privi-
leged trips will be commenced at an early day, of which public notice will
be given.

1851

A Staff for the Holy Land
Orlando B. Willcox

Through the years people suggested varying public uses for Mount Vernon, including a summer retreat for the U.S. president, an agricultural school, and an asylum for disabled and aged army and navy veterans. In 1849 Jane C. Washington quietly deeded the property to her son John, and he let it be known that the family was willing to sell the mansion and two hundred acres to the federal government—at a handsome price. In March 1851 Orlando B. Willcox of Michigan, a career army officer, accompanied President Millard Fillmore and others to the estate in order to assess its suitability as a soldiers' home. In their party was a Mr. Duncan, who was shortly to depart for the Holy Land.

This party's assessment appears in Orlando B. Willcox's *Forgotten Valor: The Memoirs, Journals, & Civil War Letters of Orlando B. Willcox*, edited by Robert Garth Scott (Kent, Oh., 1999), 175–76, and is reprinted with permission of Kent State University Press.

To-day the board of commissioners for the army asylum landed at the Fort[1] on their way over to Mount Vernon, which they were to examine with a view of selecting a site. The President of the U.S., Mr. Fillmore, & several of his cabinet—Messrs Crittenden, Hall & Stuart[2]—accompanied the Board, with a party of ladies. We fired a salute, showed them around the Fort, and Maj. Scott,[3] Dr. Edwards and myself accompanied the party to Mt. Vernon.

Mr. Augustus Washington,[4] the occupant of the place, would sell 200 acres to the Government for $200,000, on the conditions that the remains of Gen'l Washington and other members of the family should

Excursion steamboats typically stopped briefly at Fort Washington, Maryland, just upriver from Mount Vernon. Private Robert Knox Sneden, a Union soldier, produced this sketch entitled "View of Fort Washington, opposite Mount Vernon" in 1862. (Copyright 1996, Virginia Historical Society, Richmond)

not be disturbed, and that the property shall never be disposed of to private individuals. A. Col. Stockton, citizen of Florida & graduate of West Point, was with the party, and we walked around the grounds together. There was a Mr. Duncan, from New Orleans, present, who is going to the Holy Land and wished a flag staff from Mt. Vernon on which to raise the American flag on his journeys. It was selected at about 40 yards from the Tomb by our Maj. Scott; the President cut it down with an axe, which by the by he looked at & handled with the air of a woodsman, and [Maj.] Scott presented it. His tall person, as he held the staff in his hand, formed a ludicrous contrast to the figure of Mr. Duncan, a gentleman of about 5 feet. The staff was of cedar. The idea of its going to greet the Cedars of

Lebanon, of its carrying the flag of Light & Liberty back to the Land from which Light and true Liberty emanated, is rather touching.

1. Fort Washington.

2. John J. Crittenden, the attorney general; Nathan K. Hall, the postmaster general; and Alexander H. H. Stuart, the secretary of the interior.

3. Winfield Scott.

4. That is, John Augustine Washington.

1852

A Visit from Kossuth
W. T. C.

Beginning with France in 1789, the American Revolution helped inspire a wave of revolutionary movements across Europe and Latin America, but most were unsuccessful in establishing enduring democratic systems of government. Lojos Kossuth, the hero of a failed uprising in Hungary, subsequently traveled to the United States, where he had a wrenching emotional experience at Mount Vernon.

This travel account appeared in W. T. C.'s "Kossuth at Mount Vernon," *New-York Weekly Tribune* (New York City), 24 Apr. 1852.

Kossuth visited Mt. Vernon to-day. No man, of whatever country, who honors true greatness, can visit the home of Washington without reverent emotion, without earnest reflection upon the calm majesty, dignified justness and moral force of that character which swayed the destinies of America in the stormy times of our Revolution. What of Kossuth at that home?—at the Tomb of Washington? Kossuth, who might have been the Washington of Hungary but for treachery. Kossuth who pleads for his "downtrodden fatherland;" who asks from us what

This bird's-eye "View of Washington," published by E. Sachse about 1852, shows the unfinished Washington monument in the distance and, at the end of broad Pennsylvania Avenue, the White House. Across the Potomac River, Mount Vernon lies about fifteen miles to the south via the town of Alexandria.
(Courtesy of the Library of Congress)

Washington had from France, and to whom the oppressed of all Europe look in the devout hope that the success of Washington may yet be his, and their form of government that of which Washington was the first chief.—With his own oriental richness of style and poetry of imagery, the exiled Magyar could not himself reveal the emotions, regrets, resolves and hopes of this important day in his eventful history.

The party consisted of Kossuth and his wife, F. Pulszky, P. Hajnik, and Captain Grechenek, of Kossuth's suite; Senator Seward[1] and wife; Elwood Fisher, of *The Southern Press;* Rev. Mr. Bellows, of New York, and wife; Grace Greenwood, and Miss Anna Phillips, of Lynn, Mass. The boat left the Washington wharf at ten o'clock. Kossuth and party embarked at Alexandria, wither they had gone in carriages. The weather was fair, the sky unclouded, the crowd on the boat not large, and the passengers congratulated themselves upon the circumstances favoring their "pilgrimage."

The boat stopped for twenty minutes at Fort Washington. Kossuth and party visited the Fort, and by the Commander were afforded every opportunity for observation. Kossuth went into the soldiers' quarters, and examined minutely the accoutrements and the accommodations of the soldiers.

Arrived at Mt. Vernon, accompanied by Senator Seward, Mr. Pulszky, Mr. Hajnik, Grace Greenwood, and others of the ladies, Kossuth and his wife proceeded to the tomb. Kossuth stood for a few moments apparently unmoved, to those who were not near him, but those who were near him felt that he struggled to suppress emotion. In a few moments he grasped the iron railing, rested his face upon his hands, and wept—his whole frame throbbed with emotion. It was emotion which should have been unobserved, but which was too intense for even Kossuth's will to control. It was not a moment, as I consider honest human nature, for thought. The heart has the mastery in such moments—the affections control—thought comes afterward. Kossuth had aimed as Washington aimed—he renewed Washington's example—he fell—his country lies bleeding—an exile he stood at Washington's tomb—was it any wonder his frame throbbed with emotion—that he wept, and that his countrymen wept with him, as did Pulszky and Hajnik? He turned away and walked alone from the tomb—it was an hour for solitude—what were his thoughts I would not speculate.

When Kossuth returned from his sad, solitary walk he looked more melancholy than I have ever seen him. The lines on his face seemed deepened as if many years of thought had been added to his life. He was immediately met by Senator Seward, and was introduced to Mr.

This photograph captures the appearance of the mansion ca. 1858. Visitors often commented on the tree trunks that shored up the roof in place of the original columns. The balustrade on the roof and the porch to the left were added in the nineteenth century. (Courtesy of the Mount Vernon Ladies' Association)

Washington, son of the proprietor of Mount Vernon,[2] who is a grand nephew of the first President. Mr. Washington conducted the party to the mansion. Kossuth had plucked a spear of grass at Washington's tomb, which he presented to his wife. He expressed himself grieved that Mount Vernon was not the property of the Nation. Senator Seward said a public opinion was being formed which must demand a movement that would secure it as such; and Mr. Washington remarked that if the Nation ever expressed a desire, through its Representatives, to possess the spot the family would surrender it. Kossuth said he feared there was not deep piety for the dead in America—not as deep, at least, as in some other countries. He thought the memory of the illustrious dead should be cherished by nations, and the legacy of their great deeds and good example should be commemorated in proper respect and attention to the places where their remains reposed.

When Kossuth was conducted to the various rooms in the mansion he examined the furniture, pictures and relics with manifest interest. To the key of the Bastile, presented to Washington by La Fayette, he directed the attention of his wife, and spoke of it in a manner which indicated that it was to him a relic that should not be forgotten. Your readers know Kossuth was himself a prisoner for Liberty's sake in his own country.

The only room in which Kossuth was separated from the visitors generally was the library. Here none but his friends were admitted. He examined the books, and made many inquiries about Washington's habits. . . . Grace Greenwood had picked a twig of cedar from a tree near Washington's tomb. In the library she presented it to Kossuth; he accepted it with thanks, which were spoken faintly, but which were to be seen clearly in his eyes.

When the party left the library they walked through the yard, looked for a few moments at the garden and returned to the boat.

It had been an interesting reminiscence to have visited, with Kossuth, the death-bed chamber of Washington, but he was not invited to enter it.

On the return of the boat to the Capital it touched at Alexandria. A small crowd had assembled on the wharf. When the steamer left the wharf, three cheers were given by the crowd for Kossuth. He bowed to the people at each cheer.

At 3½ [o'clock] the boat reached the Washington wharf. Kossuth went with Senator Seward to his mansion, where he spent a part of the evening.

Thus ended the visit to Mount Vernon.

1. William Seward of New York.
2. Here Jane C. Washington is identified as the owner; it was not yet common knowledge that she had deeded the estate to her son.

1853

ENTER THE LADIES
Louisa Cunningham

By the early 1850s it seemed clear that Congress, no matter how much public pressure it received, would not be able to purchase Washington's home: the state of Virginia intended to exercise its right, under the Constitution, to block transfer of land within its borders to the federal government. But neither did the state act on suggestions that it acquire the property.

Because John Augustine Washington and his wife, Eleanor Love Selden Washington, wearied of their bizarre circumstances—raising a young family and trying to maintain a semblance of privacy at a place inundated by hundreds of strangers every week—John entertained thoughts of a private sale. Mere mention of this possibility aroused public anxiety, which seemed justified when rumor spread in the summer of 1853 that he had agreed to sell the heart of the estate to northern and southern investors—"capitalists." Countered one commentator, "it is not to a single private individual, or to a company of private capitalists, but to the whole American people that the sacred acres of Mount Vernon ought to belong."

A South Carolina woman named Louisa Cunningham agreed. After seeing Mount Vernon from the deck of a steamboat one night in 1853, she proposed that southern women should rescue the site for the American people. Here she writes to enlist the cooperation of Eleanor L. S. Washington. Considering her description of organizational plans already underway, as well as John A. Washington's proprietorship, the letter seems both somewhat belated and misdirected.

This letter, dated 30 December, to Eleanor L. S. Washington is among the holdings of the Mount Vernon Ladies' Association and is used with permission. The material quoted above is from "Mount Vernon," *Daily National Intelligencer* (Washington, D.C.), 28 June 1853.

A rumour has reached us, that Mt Vernon is for sale, & that an effort will be made, by a company of Northern Capitalists, to secure it; we observe that . . . Virginia, objects to its purchase by Congress, the State not being willing to relinquish its claim.

Under these circumstances, it has occurred to me, that the Ladies of the South, might effect the desirable object, of procuring this spot, which excites so deep an interest in the feelings of both Americans & foreignors, as a place of public resort, without interfering with the claims of Virginia as a State. An article has appeared in the Charleston Mercury of Decr. 2nd, making an appeal to the ladies, to organize societies & procure subscriptions, various influential persons have been addressed by letter, to enlist their sympathy, & secure their aid for this cause, in the success of which, I feel deeply interested. . . . [I]f the necessary sum can be collected, of which no doubt seems to be entertained, it would be a noble monument to our Country's benefactor, one which the daughters of the South should be proud to erect, & which I, the originator of the project will make every effort to render successful.

1854
A PROGRESS REPORT
Anonymous

It was Louisa Cunningham's daughter, Ann Pamela Cunningham, who seized the challenge and was instrumental in founding the Mount Vernon Ladies' Association. Success would depend on organizing a fund-raising

Ann Pamela Cunningham, founder of the Mount Vernon Ladies' Association.
Portrait by James Reid Lambdin, 1870.
(Courtesy of the Mount Vernon Ladies' Association)

campaign and securing John Augustine Washington's consent to sell the
site. In the same month that her mother wrote to Eleanor Love Selden
Washington, and using the pen name "Southern Matron," Ann P.
Cunningham issued an appeal to the women of the South to save the
property. Soon she agreed to seek benefactors from throughout the nation,
a practical and wise decision in view of sectional animosities. Owing to
Mount Vernon's special status as a repository of memories of the high
civic virtues, accomplishments, and heroism associated with both George
Washington and the Revolution, the task of raising several hundred thou-
sand dollars would prove remarkably easy. The association would take
possession of the mansion, tomb, and two hundred surrounding acres on
Washington's birthday in 1860.

"The Mount Vernon Purchase," an unidentified newspaper clipping (1854),
is among the Benson Lossing Papers (6646), in Special Collections at the
University of Virginia Library, Charlottesville, and is used with permission.

The brave and patriotic "Southern Matron"—(who turns out to be no
matron at all, but a noble maiden, whom Providence has made childless,
that her country may call her *mother*)[1] has fairly commenced organizing
her forces to secure from her countrywomen the balance requisite to
complete the purchase of Mount Vernon, and to adorn and preserve it as
a shrine and hallowed place for ever! To give to *all* the privilege of con-
tributing to this great and graceful deed, it is proposed that the subscriptions shall be of small sums—that they shall be collected through the
agency of committees of ladies, in each county and city of every state in
the Union, and at the head of each committee shall be a Regent, who
respectively, and as a body, shall constitute a permanent board to regu-
late and superintend the arrangements. . . . In the course of the summer
the different committees will be organized; and all political and personal interests are to be absolutely ignored in the selection of persons and

This rare image adorning the cover of *Washington's Tomb Ballad*, sheet music published in 1850, shows not only the new tomb and monuments marking the graves of nineteenth-century Washington family members but also an African American whose job it was to sell canes made from timber felled on the estate. Although some visitors harshly criticized such sales, others recognized that people who bought canes were less likely to make away with other "relics," including bits of the house, outbuildings, and fences. (Courtesy of the Virginia Historical Society, Richmond)

in subsequent action; the aim is purely patriotic—an American woman's movement in the best sense of the term.

1. Here the writer drew an overt parallel between Ann Pamela Cunningham and George Washington, who, it was said, could be the father of his country because he had no children of his own.

1856

"HOLY GROUND, SACRED PLEASURE"

Augusta Blanche Berard

When members of the extended Washington and Custis families returned to Mount Vernon in the nineteenth century, they recalled times past and also enjoyed the hospitality of the incumbent owners. More knowingly than most who journeyed to the estate, family members realized how much it had changed over the years. In April 1856 Augusta Blanche Berard, a schoolteacher from New York, visited her friend Martha Custis Williams ("Markie"). Williams lived at Arlington House, the home of her great-uncle George Washington Parke Custis, who was also the grandson and heir of Martha Washington, and who loved to reminisce about growing up at Mount Vernon. Together the two women traveled by steamboat to the estate.

This account appears in "Arlington and Mount Vernon, 1856: As Described in a Letter of Augusta Blanche Berard," *Virginia Magazine of History and Biography* 57 (1949): 155–56, 162, and is reprinted with permission.

On Friday morning Markie started with me for Mt. Vernon. We took the boat; the banks of the river are very pleasant. The most beautiful object I saw was Arlington which shows strikingly for miles. There were many people on the boat, & when we landed and followed the crowd from the wharf I thought my enjoyment would be marred. But with the exception of one shock, it was not. I felt nothing but the Sacredness of the spot. I stood at the *Tomb* of *Washington*. It was holy ground. I experienced a momentary shock as a woman uttered some pleasantry & laughed close by the grating which encloses the sarcophagus, but soon she turned away and my own feelings of sacred pleasure made me forget others. Next to the Sarcophagus beneath which rests the remains of Washington, stands another bearing this inscription "Mary [Martha] the wife of Washington." Near bye stands the monument to Mrs. Lewis,[1] an adopted daughter of Washington and an Aunt very tenderly beloved by Martha [Williams]. She felt deeply as we stood by the grave. Markie's last visit to Mt. Vernon had been with her Grandmother[2] & Uncle Custis[3] when they came to consign the dear remains of this beloved Sister to the tomb. Mrs. Lewis must have been a very remarkable and superior woman from what I can learn. Her portrait is one of the most beautiful at Arlington. Markie told me, as we walked round the Square, (as it used to be called,) the broad pathway, now overgrown with weeds, which surrounds the grounds, that her Grandmother, on that occasion, making her last visit to this home of her childhood, felt painfully the *neglect* into which everything had fallen. It is very sad. We called on Mrs. Augustine Washington.[4] A rather pretty mother & housekeeper, and looks as if she would give up Mt. Vernon to-morrow, to be delivered from the bore of visitors. We saw the Key of the Bastille presented to Washington by LaFayette on the destruction of the building. In the large room I was particularly interested in the beautiful Sienna marble mantel piece given by Dr. Vaughan's grandfather, Mr. Saml. Vaughan of London, to Genl. Washington. It is exquisitely carved, & the most perfect polish I ever saw. The figures of women & animals are admirable. I enjoyed standing by the window of the usual sitting room & whilst gazing on the fair Potomac to hear Markie repeat remarks which she had heard her Grandmother & Aunt Lewis make in & of this apartment. It had sweetest associations to both. It was the apartment in which every evening Washington met his family. . . .

[Several days later:] I enjoyed that evening a long talk with Mr. Custis about Mt. Vernon. He told me of the daily routine of life there. You know he was the adopted son of Genl. Washington. He spoke of Mrs. Washington's admirable management of her servants and household, going through every department before or immediately after breakfast. From nine o'clo[ck] until 10 o'clo every morning she retired to her *own* room for an hour of meditation reading & prayer and *that* hour no one was ever allowed to interfere with. Then her young female servants were gathered in her apartment to sew under her own supervision and they became beautiful seamstresses. Mr. C[ustis] said "bad bread was a thing entirely unknown at Mt. Vernon"; that too was mixed every night under the eye of the mistress. Immediately after breakfast Mrs. Washington gave orders for dinner, appointing certain provisions, a pr of ducks, a goose or a turkey to be laid by, to be put down in case of the arrival of company; a very necessary provision in that hospitable mansion. A ham was boiled daily. The cook who rejoiced in the name of *Hercules,* was from Mr. C's description, something of a tyrant, as well as a capital cook. The Genl. rose at 4 o'clo all the year round, donned dressing gown & slippers and going to his library lighted his own fire & read or wrote until just before breakfast, when he dressed & after that meal rode over the estate & engaged in out of doors' affairs until a half hour before dinner, which was at 3 o'clo. An hour or two of the evening he spent with his family and retired punctually at 9 o'clo. I asked Mr. Custis how he & his sisters regarded him and whether children felt at home with him. He replied that they stood in much awe of him, altho' he was kind in his manner to them. They felt they were in the presence of one, who was not to be trifled with. Their grandmother was over-indulgent.

George Washington Parke Custis, who built Arlington House on land bequeathed him by George Washington and who frequently reminisced about "the chief" and events of the Revolution. Frontispiece from *Recollections and Private Memoirs of Washington by His Adopted Son, George Washington Parke Custis* ... (New York, 1859). (Courtesy of the Mount Vernon Ladies' Association)

1. Eleanor Parke Custis Lewis, a granddaughter of Martha Washington and the mistress of Woodlawn, died in 1852.

2. Martha Custis Peter, also a granddaughter of Martha Washington and sister of Eleanor Parke Custis Lewis.

3. George Washington Parke Custis, brother of Eleanor Lewis and Martha Peter.

4. Eleanor Love Selden Washington, the wife of John Augustine Washington, who was the last family member to own Mount Vernon.

1861

HOMAGE AND ANGUISH
A Letter Written on Board the U.S. *Pawnee*

For decades ship bells tolled and crews stood at attention whenever United States naval vessels glided past Washington's home and tomb. As the Union fractured in the spring of 1861, the crew on board the gunboat U.S. Pawnee *staged a particularly solemn ceremony. On 15 April 1861, in the same issue in which this anguished letter from an unidentified crew member appeared, the* Daily National Intelligencer *announced the surrender of Union forces at Fort Sumter, South Carolina, and President Abraham Lincoln's call for seventy-five-thousand northern troops to oppose the Confederacy. The* Pawnee *was under orders to help evacuate Union troops from Fort Sumter.*

This letter was published in "Mount Vernon," *Daily National Intelligencer* (Washington, D.C.).

In passing down the Potomac river, and arriving opposite Mount Vernon, a beautiful and graceful tribute was paid to the sacred remains that lie entombed in that hallowed spot. All hands were called, officers in swords and epaulets, sailors in their neat uniform, the fine guard of the Pawnee drawn up, with belt and musket: at a given signal the large American ensign fell at half-mast, the ship's bell tolled out its muffled tones, the melancholy drums rolled their funeral salute, while the presented arms and uncovered heads of officers and men paid a sad tribute of respect to him who was "first in war, first in peace, and first in the hearts of his countrymen;" and so the Pawnee passed on silent and mourning, for he by whose grave she glided was the Father of his Country—a country scarcely a lifetime old; yet the children of the second generation are ready to tear it to pieces, and with its ruins hide forever from the eye of men that grave and all the deeds which make it so famous in the world.

Pass by this grave, oh Americans, as did the Pawnee and her gallant crew, and if after you have the hearts to rend each other, to scatter ashes and ruin over the land of Washington, then, indeed, is vain all virtue and patriotism, and the sooner the iron heel of despotism is planted firmly upon the neck of the people the better. Let both North and South remember the cry, "Those that rule by the sword shall perish by the sword."

The Pawnee goes upon her duty. She will, under the direction of her gallant commander and officers, perform it faithfully, no matter how painful it may be—no matter how many friendships may be broken, no matter how much we may differ about the right or wrong of it.

1861

SOLDIERS AND SHAWLS
Sarah Tracy

The Civil War brought thousands of Union and Confederate soldiers to the District of Columbia and northern Virginia. Some of them, dressed in military uniform and carrying guns, made pilgrimages to Mount Vernon, and that created a problem. Building on a half-century of public veneration, the Ladies' Association wanted both armies to treat the site as sacred neutral ground. In this letter Sarah Tracy, a New Yorker and the only association representative who lived at the estate during the long years of conflict, describes what proved to be a temporary solution. The letter is addressed to Ann Pamela Cunningham.

This letter, dated 20 May, to Ann Pamela Cunningham is found in *Mount Vernon: The Civil War Years,* edited by Dorothy Troth Muir (Mount Vernon,

Sarah Tracy of New York, secretary to Ann Pamela Cunningham,
lived at Mount Vernon throughout the Civil War years. In this contemporary
photograph she stands in front of the porch on the south side of the mansion.
(Courtesy of the Mount Vernon Ladies' Association)

Va., 1993), 51, and is reprinted with permission of the Mount Vernon Ladies'
Association.

Mr. Herbert[1] told the Captain of the Company of soldiers stationed near
here your wishes[2] with regard to their not coming here in uniform or
armed. They have behaved very well about it. Many of them come from
a great distance and have never been here, and have no clothes but their
uniforms. They borrow shawls and cover up their buttons and leave their
arms outside the enclosures, and never come but two or three at a time.
That is as much as can be asked of them.

1. Upton Herbert was kin to the Washington family and the hired superintendent of the site.

2. Ann Pamela Cunningham returned to South Carolina at the start of the war.

1861

WHITHER WASHINGTON?
From the *New York Times*

After Virginia seceded from the Union in April 1865, a rumor circulated that Washington's body had been stolen from his tomb. It is a testament to the mystique of the Revolution's prime hero that Union soldiers were dispatched to investigate. Dressed as civilians, they crossed the Potomac and immediately entered Confederate-held territory.

This account appeared in "A Visit to Mount Vernon. The Tomb of Washington Unmolested," *New York Times*, 26 May 1861.

In order to determine the truth or falsity of the rumor of the removal of the remains of WASHINGTON from the tomb of Mount Vernon, Gen. Sickles dispatched three messengers thither on Saturday morning. They left on horseback at 9 o'clock A.M., and crossed into Virginia. One-quarter of a mile beyond the bridge they met the first picket guard. They were mounted, and armed with breech-loading carbines, sabres and revolvers. The picket did not molest the party, as they stated they were simply travelers. Every two miles they met mounted scouts, similarly armed to the picket guard. At Alexandria they saw about six hundred troops. They were all well armed and equipped and seemed to drill well.

The party registered their names at the Mansion House, and ordered dinner to be ready at five P.M.; . . . they informed the landlord they were going to Mount Vernon, and that one of the party would leave for Europe on the following Wednesday, and was desirous of denying the infamous rumor of the removal of Washington's remains. On their departure they were questioned, and had their attention quietly attracted to the fact that one of the party was riding on a United States Government saddle. They pushed on, however, and were allowed to pass the scouts without being detained or suspected, until within about four miles of Mount Vernon.

Here they were overtaken by scouts, and ordered to halt. The scouts then informed them [that] they would accompany them, which they did. In conversation one of them stated there were 7,000 cavalry in Virginia. At one P.M. they arrived at Mount Vernon, went to the house, and then proceeded to examine the tomb. They found it had never been molested; cobwebs were on the bars of the gate, weeds had grown up from the ground in the interior of the vault, and the party received from Mr. Williamson, who was one of the scouts, and a member of the Loudon Cavalry, a certificate that they had visited the tomb, and telling pickets to pass them, as they were from the South, and were going to Washington to contradict the infamous libel on the State of Virginia.

They also visited the grounds. They met a carpenter who was engaged in repairing the house, and he stated that there had been no soldiers there. The party then left and took the outskirts of Alexandria on their way home. They were at last met by the picket near the Long Bridge and shewed the scout's pass, after being 10½ hours in the saddle, and having ridden over forty-six miles. What will the Virginians think when they learn that Mr Frost, a member of the Sixth Company New-York Seventh Regiment, Captain Van Nest, New-York Seventy-first Regiment, and Dr. A. Rawlings, of Sickles' Brigade, was the party?

1861

"WE ARE OVERRUN WITH SOLDIERS"
Mollie

War came to northern Virginia with a vengeance in the summer of 1861. In July the first Battle of Bull Run was fought within earshot of Mount Vernon, and Sarah Tracy reported hearing constant cannon fire. With Union troops occupying Alexandria and with Confederate picket lines established near the estate, venturing forth could prove dangerous. The writer of this letter was probably Mary McMakin, a friend of Tracy's who arrived from Philadelphia in October 1861 for a long visit.

Mollie [Mary McMakin?] wrote this letter to Caroline L. Rees on 21 and 23 October 186[1], and it is now among the Kirby Family Letters (7786-W), in Special Collections at the University of Virginia Library, Charlottesville; it is used with permission.

I am daily becoming more at home and have nothing to complain of in my external circumstances. Mr Herbert, the Superintendent a pleasant *Virginia gentleman* of 40 or more & Miss Tracy, with myself make up the *parlor circle* & Emily (cook), Priscilla (chambermaid) Frances (charity maid of all work) George (coachman & general assistant) with the gardener and one or two other hands employed about the grounds, make up the "Kitchen Cabinet." Our chief distress is the necessity of driving 8 miles to Alexandria for the mails & whatever shopping is necessary, which takes so much time as to be accomplished only once or twice a week as the men can not be oftener spared. . . . We are overrun with soldiers who come to see the place but they are generally very good & behave with becoming respect. Occasionally officers, "drest in a little brief authority" are impertinent but privates rarely. Gen. Richardson's

"A Scouting Party at Mount Vernon," by A. R. Ward for *The New-York Illustrated News*, 16 Dec. 1861, pictures Union soldiers below the old tomb and the summer house. (Courtesy of the Mount Vernon Ladies' Association)

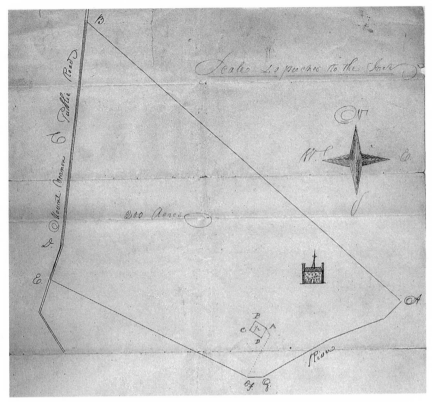

In 1853, after John Augustine Washington decided to sell the historically important core of his inheritance, he had this survey map drawn. A few years later he sold these two hundred acres to the Mount Vernon Ladies' Association. (Courtesy of the Mount Vernon Ladies' Association)

Brigade is stationed near us in the country around but the pickets are past us[1] and we do not need to show our passes but once on the way to town. I can hardly get used to the cannonading that is so distinctly heard from the various points below us on the river as the Confederate batteries fire *into* the passing vessels and receive their fire in return. It does seem so sad & so useless & while everything is so sweet and peaceful here, forces with harsh unwelcomeness the miserable conflict of human passions on one's mind. . . .

Wed, 23d. It rained dismally all yesterday and I sewed & read & knitted leaving the evening to write to you, but our masculine companion read [poli]tical speeches from the N. Y. & Missouri papers to us aloud and I sewed & listened. The sun is shining fitfully today and we hope the roads will be dry enough to drive to town tomorrow.

1. That is, a Union picket line at this time was located south of Mount Vernon.

1862

"VANDALS LOOKING FOR RELICS"
Private Robert Knox Sneden

In March 1862 Private Robert Knox Sneden was assigned to a reconnaissance mission that took him from the Union lines near Alexandria, where he was stationed, southward into Prince William County, Virginia. Confederate forces had recently withdrawn from the area. Sneden's diary captures the desolation and ravage already caused by the war. En route back to Alexandria he made a detour to Mount Vernon, where he discovered that, while the estate fared far better than the surrounding neighborhood, it was not untouched.

This diary excerpt appears in *Eye of the Storm: A Civil War Odyssey,* edited by Charles F. Bryan Jr. and Nelson D. Lankford (New York, 2000), 22–23, and is reprinted with permission of the Virginia Historical Society, Richmond.

Many houses on the road were entirely deserted. Fences were few. No live cattle of any kind were seen. Doors were hanging by one hinge and the whole country looked deserted everywhere outside the villages of Col-

Robert Knox Sneden, a private in the Union army, visited or passed by
Mount Vernon several times during the war. This watercolor entitled
"Ruins of Old Gate Lodges back of Mt. Vernon Estate" dates from 1861.
(Copyright 1996, Virginia Historical Society, Richmond)

chester and Accotink. This last village has a preponderance of Union
Quaker folks. The people seemed poor, as no business of any kind was
doing. Fishing and raising corn is all that the inhabitants can do. Not
more than 200 people were in the town who turned out in the streets to
see us pass through.

I left the escort and revisited Mount Vernon on our homeward march.
Two of us rode over a greater portion of the estate. We did not go through
the house, but entered our names on the register book in the grand hall.
We then visited both tombs and also gathered leaves to press for mementoes. Got some large acorns.

I noticed now that the carved marble eagle which was on the lid of the
sarcophagus had been broken off and carried away by some vandal looking for relics! These wretches spare nothing sacred or profane so long as

they can get a relic of some sort. The only way that I saw for the wretch to obtain the eagle was to thrust the butt end of his musket through the open barred grating of the arched entrance and break off the emblem from the face of the slab. No one could climb into the chamber as the iron spike heads of the gate went up to within a foot of the center of the arched door. The claws of the eagle remained on the slab but the remainder had vanished. I was here last [December] when everything in and about the tomb were intact. The custodian of the estate at the mansion did not know of this vandalism until I informed him of it. He does not go over the grounds very often, as he stands a chance at night especially, of being shot by either our or Rebel pickets who sometimes are on the grounds prowling around after something of use while in camp.

1865

"WE BELIEVE THE PLACE WHERE WE ARE STANDING TO BE HOLY"
George W. Clymans

On 11 May 1865 George W. Clymans, who belonged to a Pennsylvania regiment and had recently arrived in Virginia after Sherman's march through Georgia, walked to Mount Vernon. Accompanying him that day were other Union soldiers. Thus men who had helped preserve the Union came to pay homage to the person most influential in creating it. The mood was somber. The war had ended, and Abraham Lincoln had been assassinated the previous month.

This journal account, entitled "A Visit to Mount Vernon," is among the holdings of the Mount Vernon Ladies' Association and is used with permission.

Accompanied by some of my comrades of the 205th, we left our camp near Alexandria at 8 o'clock A.M. and after walking perhaps four or five miles in a South-eastern direction we reached the Mt. Vernon estate.

"View of the Mansion at Mount Vernon," by Robert Knox Sneden, 1861.
Sneden probably sketched this view from memory, for it contains several inaccuracies,
including the height of rooflines and the appearance of the old tomb.
(Copyright 1996, Virginia Historical Society, Richmond)

Entering the carriage road leading to the mansion, we wound our way amid the woods and fields, while here and there we would catch a glimpse of the majestic Potomac flowing onward to the sea.

The mansion can not be seen until you are close to it, and stands embowered amid a grove of stately old trees, the greater part of them planted by Washington himself.

We reach the lawn gate, and, after paying an entrance fee of twenty-five cents we are admitted into the grounds; passing up the nicely graveled walk we stand in front of the house in which lived and died the immortal Washington.

We are here met by the gentleman[1] who occupys the mansion and has overage of the estate, who politely informed us that our best plan would

be to visit the tomb of Washington and his wife, the landing, flower garden and other objects of curiosity before entering the house.

Taking a path which led in a southerly direction (for, I suppose fifty
yards) we turned to the right, and walking a few paces in a westward
direction, we came to the vault which contains the mortal remains of
Washington and Martha his wife.

At the entrance are two gates formed of iron rods some four inches
apart, and through which you can gaze upon the sarcophagus within. Its
shape is that of a coffin, raised about a foot from the earth and resting in
a block of granite of the same shape. On the lid of Washington's coffin an
eagle is carved, holding in its claws a bunch of arrows;[2] on its breast is a
shield with the stars and stripes carved upon it.

On the small end of the sarcophagus is the following inscription: "By
the permission of Lawrence Lewis, the surviving executor of Washington, this sarcophagus was presented by John Struthers, of Philadelphia,
Marble-mason, A.D. 18[3]7." On the top of it is carved in large capitals
"Washington."

That of Martha the wife of the General is similar to his with the exception of the eagle and shield, and bears the following inscription "Martha
wife of the General." Just at the head of the coffins a marble slab is
sunken in the wall of the vault (which is of brick) on which is inscribed
the 25 & 26th verses of the 11th chapter of St John, which reads as follows: "Jesus saith unto her, I am the resurrection, and the life: he that
bel[ie]veth in me, though he were dead, yet shall he Live; and whosoev-
er Liveth and bel[ie]veth in me shall never die. Bel[ie]veth then this!"

The floor of the vault is covered with small white pebbles, of which I
brought away a few as mementoes.

In front of the vault is a monument erected to the memory of Judge
Bushrod Washington and his wife, (who survived him but two days.) The
judge was a resident of Philadelphia.[3] There is also a monument to

Washington's adopted daughter,[4] and one to Augustine Washington[5]—the inscriptions I do not remember.

The place where the great Hero's remains now rest, is where he requested to be laid, but his last wishes were not carried out after his demise and he was placed in the family vault, which is about sixty paces east of the one in which he now rests, but of that anon.

Plucking a few leaves as a memento of the place, from a tree overshading the tomb, we retrace our steps to the main path.

We take a path that leads us to the banks of the Potomac, and gaze forth upon its glancing waters, white with the sails of passing vessels. Upon the opposite side we can see the green hills of Maryland, and our eyes take in at a glance the river for miles below. Here is the pier where passing steamers land visitors for Mt. Vernon. After gazing upon the river and the passing vessels, we retrace our steps to the main walk, and passing up the steep ascent take a side path to the right, and find ourselves at the old family vault in which Washington was first laid, and where he remained until the year 1832, when his remains were removed to the new vault. It was here that in the year 182[4], Layfaette visited the tomb of his brother in arms, and after whom he (Layfaette) named a son.[6] It is close on the river's bank and is shaded by several stately old trees.

Leaving the vault we wend our way toward the mansion; stoping (when near the house of his Butler) to gather a few leaves from a stately Magnolia, which our polite attendant informed us had been planted by the General. It is a beautiful tree with leaves resembling those of the Laurel, but much larger; and appears to be dying. Coming up the Lawn walk we again stand in front of the mansion. On each side of the lawn stand the houses of the domestics formerly attached to the establishment, which are large and very comfortable habitations.

I will try to give a faint description of the outward appearance of the building. It is, I suppose, one hundred feet in length by forty in breadth;

two stories high, and built on an original style of architecture, slightly resembling the Gothic in appearance. It appears as if there had originally been a house built with the gables east and west, and that two wings had afterward been added to it with gables North and South. There are three doors fronting on the Lawn (which is south of the house) one being the main entrance and one in each of the wings. The house is weather boarded, and sanded, squares being cut so as to resemble stone.

On the roof of the main building is a cupalo with glass windows, on the top of which is a weathercock with letters on rods showing the points of the Compass. Over the main entrance is the Keystone, a circle representing the various states of the union, there being sixteen at the time the house was built.

The lower range of windows are large, while those above are exceedingly small, and present quite a contrast to those below.

There is a large brass knocker on the hall door, which we pull, and are admitted by a servant into the hall. To the right (on entering) is a table on which is a book for those to sign who wish to become members of the association, and a box to contain their subscription, which is one dollar.

Above the table hangs a glass case which contains the Key of the Bastile—a celebrated state prison of France, which was destroyed by the people of Paris during the Revolution of 178[9]. This Key was presented to General Washington by the Marquis De Lafayette.

Leaving the hall we pass into the West parlour, a room probably 15 x 18 ft in size. In one corner is the fire-place; above it hangs a painting, representing a scene in the West India Islands. Two ships of war are anchored in a bay, while in the distance is seen a mountain h[e]ight.

This painting shows the scene of a naval battle in which Lawrence Washington was engaged under the command of admiral Vernon, and after whom Lawrence named his plantation.

At his death Lawrence bequeathed Mt. Ver[n]on to George.

Old Mount Vernon, Eastman Johnson's somber view of the north side
of the mansion and some of its outbuildings, was painted in 1857.
(Courtesy of the Fraunces Tavern Museum, New York, N.Y.)

The ceiling of this room is frescoed in a very tasteful manner, but some sacrilegious hands have broken portions of it off and carried it away probably as relics. From this room we pass into the West dining room, which is a room 20 x 30 ft in size, and lighted by five windows; one of them being a large bay window in the North end, ten feet high by six wide. The first object that strikes our attention on entering this room is a Harpsichord, manufactured in London and presented to Elinor (Mrs Lewis,) Washington's adopted [grand]daughter, on her wedding day. Passing the large window we come to a side-table on which is placed the camp equipage and holsters of the General, used by him during the revolution; they are not in a very good state of preservation, and look as if they had seen hard service. Turning from these relics we stand before the mantlepiece, which is a magnificent piece of sculpture both in design and execution; carved from Carrara marble with designs in relief.

The first scene represents a farmer leaning on the handles of his plow, while the horses stand with drooping heads and ears, looking fatigued and weary; behind him is shown the fruits of his labours. All parts of this design shows the hand of a master and is carved to life.

The next is the Shepherd and his flock; there is the old sheep tossing his bell while the lambs are skipping and playing on the green bank; all as natural as life—it could not be more so. The last scene represents a woman drawing water from a well with one hand, while the other is grasping that of a child. The little babe is holding a piece of bread up to the view of a large mastiff, who has thrown himself upon his hind legs, and seems begging for the tempting morsel which the child keeps well out of his reach, and appears in no hurry to relinquish. The expression of the woman, babe and dog appears so natural that one almost imagines we are gazing on living beings, and not the senseless marble. This piece of sculpture was executed in Italy, and presented by Mr Vaughn,[7] consul at Rome, during the time Washington was president.

Taking a view from one of the east windows, of the Potomac, and fort Washington; we return to the hall and pass out on the porch on the eastern side of the building, where we can see the river for miles above and below.

Returning to the hall, we ascend the stairs to the room in which he died. Uncovering our heads as we enter, we feel awed into silence, for we believe the place where we are standing to be holy; we look around the room in which the great and good George Washington breathed his last. A bed is standing in one corner of the room; not the one on which he died but on which he frequently slept. It is a plain cherry beadstead, with slats and high posts intended for curtains. There is a Franklin stove in the room on the back plate of which is the initials of his name.

We pass into his dressing room, which is very small, being nothing more than a closet with a few shelves in the side of the room. Gazing out of the window, we have a view of the Lawn, and in the distance the lodge gate some two hundred yards off.

From this window he could see the approach of visitors, and be prepared to receive them. Turning from the window, we descend the stairway, pass out through the hall and again stand upon the Lawn in front of the mansion. But the flower garden is yet to be seen. The gardener conducts us to it, and unlocking the gate we pass in. It is a beautiful place laid out in pleasant walks bordered with boxwood hedges.

It contains every flower found on this continent, and also many foreign plants. The greater part of the flowers are in full bloom, and the air is filled with their perfume. I plucked a few buds and flowers, as mementoes of my visit; after spending an hour in the garden we returned to the house. We turn our footsteps to the old summer house, where he spent his leisure hours during the summer.[8] It is fast falling to decay, and will soon be in ruins. We seat ourselves in the same seat where Washington has sat and gaze upon the same noble river and distant hills. A feeling of sadness steals over us, as we think that perhaps we may never gaze upon these scenes again, and with feelings of pleasure and pain we take our departure. We have seen the place where our beloved and venerated Washington's remains repose.

A visit to Mt. Vernon is one which will never be regretted by a lover of his country.

As an illustration of the respect in which his name is held, the gentleman in charge of the estate mentioned, that during the time the estate was in posession of the Rebels, they never disturbed anything; not even burning a rail.

We returned to camp about 5 o'clock P.M. very tired but much pleased with our visit.

1. Upton Herbert.

2. By comparing George W. Clymans's account with that of Robert Knox Sneden, one can infer that either one man erroneously described the condition of the carved eagle or that it had been repaired by the time of Clymans's visit in 1865. Dennis J. Pogue, of the Mount Vernon staff, has found no physical evidence that would confirm Sneden's statement.

3. BW lived in Philadelphia when the Supreme Court was in session there.

4. Eleanor Parke Custis Lewis.

5. John Augustine Washington, the owner between 1829 and 1832.

6. George Washington Lafayette.

7. Samuel Vaughan.

8. Clymans was mistaken. The summer house dated from Bushrod Washington's tenure.

The Washingtons of Mount Vernon

George Washington (1732–99) inherited Mount Vernon from his half-brother Lawrence and began farming there in the 1750s, shortly before he married Martha Dandridge Custis (1731–1802). During his lifetime he expanded the estate from the twenty-three hundred acres he inherited to approximately eight thousand acres.

Before his death in 1799, Washington arranged that his nephew Lawrence Lewis and his wife, Eleanor Parke Custis Lewis (Martha Washington's granddaughter), would receive two thousand acres, on which they subsequently built Woodlawn. In his will Washington gave his wife a lifetime interest in the estate, after which the remaining six thousand acres would be divided among Bushrod Washington (1762–1829), who was the son of Washington's brother John Augustine Washington (1736–87), and George Fayette Washington and Lawrence [Charles] Augustine Washington, who were the orphaned children of Washington's nephew George Augustine Washington (1758–93). In the will Washington stated that the bequest to Bushrod was "partly in consideration of an intimation to his deceased father while we were Bachelors, & he had kindly undertaken to superintend my Estate during my Military Services in the former War between Great Britain & France [1756–63], that if I should fall therein, Mount Vernon (then less extensive in domain than at present) should become his property." The bequest to the orphaned sons of George Augustine Washington reflected "the affection I had for, and the obligation I was under to, their father when living, who from his youth had attached himself to my person, and followed my fortunes through the viscissitudes of the late Revolution— afterwards devoting his time to the Superintendence of my private concerns for many years, whilst my public employments rendered it impracticable for me to do it myself."[1]

Bushrod Washington's portion of Mount Vernon, about four thousand acres, included the mansion, to which he and his wife, Julia Ann Blackburn Washington (d. 1829), moved after Martha Washington's death. She was the daughter of Thomas Blackburn of Prince William County, Virginia, who had served in the War for Independence.[2]

When Bushrod and Julia Ann Washington died childless within days of each other in 1829, the mansion and original Washington family tomb plus 1,225 acres of land descended to Bushrod's nephew John Augustine Washington. He died in 1832, leaving the property to his wife, Jane Charlotte Blackburn Washington, the niece of Julia Ann Blackburn Washington. When Jane's eldest son, John Augustine Washington (1821-61), came of age, she turned over to him the active management of the estate. Soon thereafter he married Eleanor Love Selden of Leesburg, Virginia, and the couple made Mount Vernon their home. For her part, Jane C. Washington took up permanent residence at Blakeley, in Jefferson County, Virginia, but continued to visit Mount Vernon until her death in 1855.[3]

By then John Augustine Washington was actively trying to escape the pressures and inconveniences caused by the crush of visitors to the site; on 22 February 1860 he turned over possession of the core two hundred acres to the Mount Vernon Ladies' Association, while retaining ownership of the remaining 1,025 acres. He and his family removed to Waveland in Fauquier County, Virginia, an estate that he purchased with part of the proceeds of sale of the Mount Vernon site. Eleanor Love Selden Washington died in 1860, her husband the following year.[4]

1. Will of G. Washington [9 July 1799], in *The Papers of George Washington: Retirement Series,* ed. W. W. Abbot et al., 4 vols. (Charlottesville, Va., 1998–99), 4:479, 487–88.

2. Jean B. Lee, "Jane C. Washington, Family, and Nation at Mount Vernon, 1830–55," in *Women Shaping the South: Creating and Confronting Change,* ed. Angela Boswell and Judith McArthur (Columbia: University of Missouri Press, 2005).

3. Ibid.

4. Lee, unpublished research.